Reader's Digest · National Trust

Nature Notebooks

SEASIDE AND MOORLAND BIRDS

Reader's Digest · National Trust

Nature Notebooks

SEASIDE AND MOORLAND BIRDS

Published by The Reader's Digest Association Limited, London,
in association with The National Trust

Additional editorial work by Duncan Petersen Publishing Limited,
5 Botts Mews, London W2 5AG.
Typesetting by Modern Reprographics Limited, Hull, North
Humberside.
Separations by Modern Reprographics Limited, (covers) and
Mullis Morgan Limited, London (duplicate film).
Printed by Everbest Printing Company Limited, Hong Kong.

The illustration on the cover is of the Farne Islands
by Michael Woods.

CONTENTS

Using This Book	6-7
Identifying Birds: Basic Fieldcraft	8-10
The Birds	11-95
The Sites	96-119
Understanding Birds and Recording Techniques	119-21
Glossary	122
Index	124
Acknowledgements	127

Using this book

You are never very far from the sea in Britain, nor indeed from moorland; both are specialized, demanding habitats, and both have singular and fascinating bird populations. This book embraces both habitats in the widest sense: every type of coastal terrain is covered, from salt-marsh and mud-flats through rocky beaches to offshore islands; likewise, 'moorland' covers a wide range of interesting territory, much of it upland, and indeed some very high, positively mountainous country. In such areas, forest is often inescapably part of the scene along with conventionally open moorland terrain, so you will find quite a few wooded sites, too. The only type of 'moorland' excluded is lowland heath: some of the notable examples of this habitat in Britain are featured in a companion title in the *Nature Notebook* series: *River, Wetland and Lowland Birds*.

This book not only enables you to identify, and learn about seaside and moorland birds, but lists sites where you may be able to see them. The field guide section, pages 12-95, works hand-in-hand with the sites gazetteer, pages 96-119, by means of the panel on each field guide page. The panel includes a brief general note on each species – often describing the bird's nest. A nest affords the naturalist an excellent opportunity for watching and identifying birds, but we would stress how essential it is not to approach too close to the nest.

Below the caption we list a sequence of numbers directing you to sites described in the gazetteer, in all of which you have an excellent chance of seeing the bird in question. They are not the *only* sites in the book where you will see it, but they are the most interesting

ones. Equally, you will find some species cross-referenced to a site, but not mentioned in the site description: this is because space in the gazetteer tends to allow mention only of selected, key species.

In certain cases, comparisons are made between the appearance or habits of a seaside or moorland bird and those of a bird not included in this book. This is for the benefit of those who may possess the two other books in this series: *River, Wetland and Lowland Birds* and *Garden and Woodland Birds.*

The selection of species
The 84 birds chosen for the field guide section are by no means all the seaside and moorland/upland birds that can be seen in Britain; however, they are a representative selection of the most familiar of such species, and they are the most likely to be seen by the visitor without local knowledge. Among them are a fair sprinkling of uncommon birds, but also birds which, though rare on a nationwide basis, can easily be seen if you visit the site which specializes in them. Where no specific sites are mentioned, the bird is either so common that it can be seen at the majority of sites, or so rare that its nesting areas are deliberately kept secret.

The selection of sites
The places described for bird-watching in the gazetteer section are, in England and Wales, mainly National Trust property. They have the excellent advantage of generally easy access, though it should also be realized that much of the land is not for the public to roam freely. Viewing is in many places

from roads only, or from footpaths and tracks which are public rights of way. For this reason, a large scale map such as the Ordnance Survey Landranger sheet (scale 1:50 000) is extremely useful since it shows footpaths which are public rights of way.

The Scottish and Irish sites are in some cases managed by the National Trust for Scotland; otherwise they are nature reserves or bird sanctuaries to which the public generally has easy access – without membership of an organization or possessing a special permit. In addition to the National Trust sites in England and Wales, there are also featured a number of first-class properties owned or managed by other bodies: these are intended to make the coverage more comprehensive, both in terms of geographical spread and of species.

The panel for notes
The space at the foot of each colour plate on pages 12-95 is a convenient introduction to the excellent – some would say essential – habit of making notes of bird observations. Individual headings are given for all the most important types of information needing to be logged when seeing a bird: location, time of day, weather, behaviour, and so on; but most important of all is the blank space left free for a sketch. However feeble you believe your artistic efforts may be, they are always worth making: a sketch forces you to recall, or to note specific aspects of a bird in detail.

The colour plates
The superb bird illustrations on pages 12-95 give you not only close-up, but also distant views of every species, and

this is of course invaluable for identification.

There are sometimes marked differences between the plumages of males and females of the same species, or between their winter and summer or adult and juvenile plumages. All the main plumage variations which occur during a bird's stay in Britain are illustrated.

The distribution maps

The map on each colour plate shows you when and where you are most likely to see the species. The time of year when you see a bird, or the part of Britain where you see it, can be useful clues to identification.

Red dots show the sites of breeding colonies.

Red shading shows the usual breeding range of summer visitors.

Green shows the usual breeding range of species present in Britain all year round.

Blue shows the areas where a species is found in winter.

Shading indicates where passage migrants occur – those species which stop in Britain while moving to or from breeding or wintering grounds outside the British Isles.

THE NATIONAL TRUST AND ITS WORK

The National Trust, a private charity founded in 1895, can claim to be the oldest conservation organization in the country. As well as caring for historic houses, castles and gardens, it owns 500,000 acres of land throughout England, Wales and Northern Ireland. With such extensive holdings it is not surprising that it owns many superb examples of each of the main habitat types in Britain: coasts, woods, moorlands, uplands, heaths, grasslands, lakes, rivers and mires. It acquired its first nature reserve, Wicken Fen, as early as 1895, and by 1910 had 13 properties of particular wildlife value. It now owns some 90 nature reserves, over 400 Sites of Special Scientific Interest (SSSIs) and many other properties of great interest, not only for birds, but for plants and animals.

The National Trust for Scotland, a separate organization, but with similar aims and objectives, was established in 1931 and owns 100,000 acres, including some of the finest mountain and coastal scenery.

The Royal Society for the Protection of Birds (RSPB) and the Royal Society for Nature Conservation (RSNC) which, like the National Trusts, are charities with no direct government funding, have also been actively involved in wildlife conservation for many decades. The RSPB was founded in 1889 and manages over a hundred Reserves covering 130,000 acres. The RSNC, established in 1912, acts as a national association for 46 Nature Conservation Trusts which between them manage Nature Reserves covering 1,120,000 acres.

Coasts, moorlands and uplands are the best-represented habitats on Trust property. Over four hundred miles of coast-line is owned by the National Trust, much of which has been acquired through the Enterprise Neptune Appeal which was launched in 1965 after it had been established that one-third of the coastline of England and Wales was developed and spoilt beyond redemption. In the uplands, enormous tracts have been transferred or given to the Trust.

One of the particular concerns of the National Trust in managing the coastal and upland properties important for breeding birds is to ensure that the nesting birds are not disturbed by the public. Terns and ringed plover nesting on open ground on sand and shingle are susceptible to trampling damage and disturbance by people and dogs; and cliff- or crag-nesting seabirds and birds of prey can be disturbed by rock climbers.

The Trust employs over two hundred wardens and additional seasonal staff, and careful wardening of nesting sites is an important part of their duties in the Lake District, the Peak District and for the Norfolk and Northumberland tern colonies, for instance. Boat trips to the Farne Islands are scheduled to only two of the islands and the visitors keep to prescribed routes.

These are but a few examples of the National Trust's extremely varied bird conservation activities; visiting the immensely-varied range of coastal and upland properties described in this book is in the end the only way to properly appreciate the diversity of British upland and coastal birds, and to understand something of their specific habitat requirements and the efforts, care and resources which go into National Trust property management.

Katherine Hearn,
Assistant Adviser on Conservation,
The National Trust.

Identifying Birds: Basic Fieldcraft

To identify birds successfully, you need to concentrate your powers of observation on several distinct aspects of a given species. Probably the two most important are distinguishing, or diagnostic, field marks, and relative size. The pictures and captions on pages 9 and 10 will help you get to grips with these basic concepts. Of course, you will also need to be aware of, and observe, overall plumage colour, bill shape and size, flight pattern, song and behaviour. Building up a working knowledge of these is largely a matter of experience; and of capitalizing on that experience by taking notes – see page 6.

But clearly, if you are too far away from a bird to see or hear it, all the ornithological knowledge in the world is of little practical value. Fieldcraft is the art of being in the right place at the right time, so that you are close enough to make a positive identification, either on the spot, or later with the help of notes and a field guide.

Fieldcraft starts before you even leave home on a bird-watching trip: time spent in planning and preparation is never wasted. Check the weather report: forecasts of rain or poor visibility could mean disappointment. Plan your journey so that, if possible, you arrive at your destination early – song is a valuable clue, and is at its loudest early in the day.

Before leaving you should also think about clothing and footwear suitable for the trip. Choose inconspicuous clothes in camouflage colours, rather than bright hues which attract attention. Try also to find clothing that does not rustle – some garments made from artificial fibre make a noise each time you move.

Use footwear that is suited to the terrain you are visiting: gum boots are ideal for mud-flats, but provide less grip than plimsolls when scrambling over boulders, and make heavy work of walking through loose sand dunes.

Though you can often identify a bird with the naked eye, binoculars make the process much easier. When choosing a pair, look for the two engraved numbers – such as 10 × 50. The smaller number indicates magnification; the larger number, the lens diameter, and thus the light-gathering power of the binoculars. For the novice bird-watcher, 8 × 30s are a sound first choice. They are easy to focus, gather sufficient light even for use at dusk, and are not too heavy to carry round all day. Before buying a pair, though, it is wise to try other people's binoculars and see which you prefer.

In the field

Once you are on the spot, it almost goes without saying that you should aim to be as inconspicuous as possible. If you are visiting a small area, start by doing a brief survey of the site before choosing somewhere to settle down. In upland areas, for example, a spot that provides views of the edge of a wood, across a boggy area and up towards a crag is a more promising place to watch from than somewhere that looks out across just one kind of habitat.

Being inconspicuous can mean literally concealing yourself in the shelter of a wall or fence, but you might be surprised at how little cover is needed to deceive a bird. The strong lines of a five-bar gate, for example, are often enough to disguise your human outline – provided you keep still. Thin undergrowth can be equally effective.

Often there is no such convenient cover, but you can avoid drawing unnecessary attention to yourself by standing against a background which is roughly the same tone as your clothing: at the foot of chalk cliffs, position yourself at the mouth of a cave, not against the white rock face. In upland areas, keep off the horizon.

If you plan to walk some distance, you'll want to get a move on, but more birds will be visible if you make regular stops, keeping still for five to ten minutes. In constant motion yourself, it is easy to miss the small movements in undergrowth that can alert you to the presence of birdlife. Additionally, birds are less frightened by static observers, and will come closer to you. If you suspect that there are birds around, but that they will not emerge from cover, try making a noise; but in the breeding season, don't go beating through the undergrowth – this could easily disturb ground-nesting birds.

Use your eyes and ears to locate bird life, and pay attention not only to the birds themselves but the clues they leave behind – a wader's footprints in mud, or the stain of droppings down the favourite crag of a peregrine.

Coastal tips

If you are visiting the coast or an estuary, tide is an important factor in planning a trip. Where there is mud, the best time to visit is soon after high tide; waders are then concentrated close to the shore on the narrow bands of ooze. As the tide falls, they have more area on which to feed, and will move some distance away from dry land.

Maps are of inestimable value when

Knowing what to look for is the key to success in identifying birds. The size, shape and colouring of a bird are the first and most obvious clues to its identity. But how it stands or moves, how it swims or flies, how it sings, feeds or approaches its mate – these and other aspects of its behaviour may be just as distinctive as its plumage. The time of year, and the place where the bird is seen, are also identification points. Some birds only visit Britain at particular times of the year, coming from breeding or wintering grounds that may be thousands of miles away. Other birds are so well adapted to life in a particular habitat that they are only rarely encountered outside it.

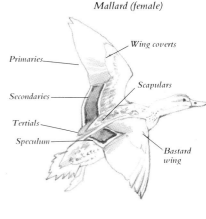

Mallard (female)

Primaries

Wing coverts

Secondaries

Scapulars

Tertials

Speculum

Bastard wing

Oystercatcher

Wing-bar

Rump

Terminal band

House sparrow (male)

Crown

Forehead

Ear coverts

Beak

Nape

Chin

Back

Throat

Breast

Rump

Upper tail coverts

Tail

Supercilium

Eye-ring

Moustachial stripe

Belly

Flanks

Tarsus

Under tail coverts

Hind claw

Toes

Reed bunting (female)

Naming the parts

Putting the right name to the parts of a bird is almost as important as naming the bird itself. For it provides a language in which to discuss birds with other birdwatchers, and it makes for quick and simple note-taking in the field.

searching for new places to observe sea-birds. The 1:50 000 Landranger series of Ordnance Survey maps mark most important coastal features, with individual symbols to identify slopes, cliff, flat rock, sand and mud, sand and shingle, and high and low water marks. Look especially for headlands and islands: standing on them during the breeding season, you can turn back towards the mainland to see cliff-nesting birds; looking out to sea, there is a better chance of seeing true sea-birds such as petrels; and during spring and autumn, birds in passage favour an island or headland for landfalls.

Pay attention to safety on the coast: even in apparently harmless areas it is easy to forget the time and get cut off by the tide. Two of the sites listed in the gazetteer at the back of the book are reached by a causeway that is covered by the rising tide, and misreading the tide-tables is potentially disastrous at these spots. Salt-marsh can be dangerous, too – the water can rise very quickly in the muddy tidal creeks that snake through

What size is it?

When an unfamiliar bird is seen, the first point to note is its size. The easiest way to fix this is by comparing it with a bird that is known. Measured from its bill tip to the tip of its tail, for instance, a house sparrow is 5¾ in. (14·5 cm), while a blackbird is nearly twice as long, at 10 in. (25 cm). The familiar mallard is twice as long again, at 23 in. (58 cm), while its frequent companion on the waters of rivers and lakes, the mute swan, is the largest of all British birds, at 60 in. (152 cm) in length. The shape of a bird can also be very distinctive. For instance, it may be slim and delicate like a wagtail, or plump and stocky like a wood-pigeon.

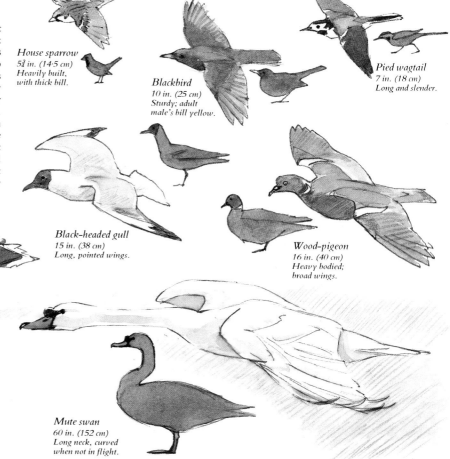

House sparrow
5¾ in. (14·5 cm)
Heavily built,
with thick bill.

Blackbird
10 in. (25 cm)
Sturdy; adult
male's bill yellow.

Pied wagtail
7 in. (18 cm)
Long and slender.

Black-headed gull
15 in. (38 cm)
Long, pointed wings.

Wood-pigeon
16 in. (40 cm)
Heavy bodied;
broad wings.

Mallard
23 in. (58 cm)
Stout bodied;
long wings.

Mute swan
60 in. (152 cm)
Long neck, curved
when not in flight.

some saltings. Take special care on cliffs, and don't go near unstable edges.

Moorland and upland tips

Watching moorland and upland birds is more of a challenge than scanning the coast-line. Concentrations of birds are usually lower, and in some areas you can walk all day and see only a handful of curlews. However, for many enthusiasts, the glimpse of a bird of prey soaring majestically over a crag more than makes up for the relative scarcity of other birdlife.

Safety first is the rule on high moors, fells and peaks, even if the danger is not immediately apparent. If you are stranded alone with a broken ankle, it does not matter whether the nearest road is half-a-mile away, or ten miles. Always walk with other people, never by yourself. Three is the safest practical minimum – if one is hurt, the second stays on the spot while number three fetches help.

Always let someone know your route and estimated time of return. And having done that, don't vary the route.

SEASIDE AND MOORLAND BIRDS

An identification guide to 84 species

●

The species are grouped by family, starting with the more primitive families and ending with the most advanced species. For some basic advice on identifying birds, see pages 8-10; for further information on bird classification, see pages 119-20.

●

If you already know the name of a species and want to look it up, simply consult the index.

●

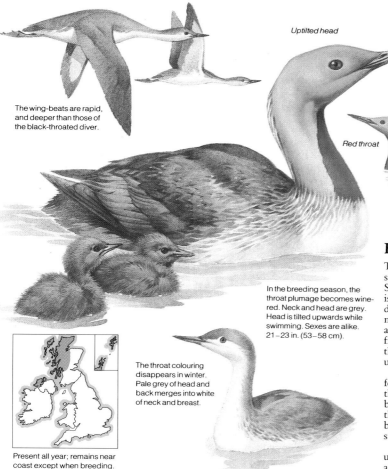

The wing-beats are rapid, and deeper than those of the black-throated diver.

Uptilted head

Red throat

A bird on the alert swims low in the water. Its throat-patch looks dark unless seen in a bright light.

In the breeding season, the throat plumage becomes wine-red. Neck and head are grey. Head is tilted upwards while swimming. Sexes are alike. 21–23 in. (53–58 cm).

The throat colouring disappears in winter. Pale grey of head and back merges into white of neck and breast.

Present all year; remains near coast except when breeding.

SITES GUIDE

The nests of the red-throated diver are heaps of moss or water plants, usually in offshore shallows or on land at the water's edge.

The species may be seen at sites numbers: 2, 9, 10, 17, 18, 30, 35, 44, 45, 52, 56, 65.

Red-throated diver *Gavia stellata*

The red-throated diver is a good swimmer both on or below the surface, and one of only four species of diver in the world. Superbly streamlined, neck outstretched and legs tucked back, it is also graceful in flight. Alas, like all divers, it is somewhat at a disadvantage on landing: its legs, so well adapted for swimming, are set far back on its body, giving the bird a most awkward gait. But so efficient is it under water that it can chase fish or scoop up shellfish as deep as 30 ft (9 m). And so fast is it on the surface that a courting bird may 'run' on the water, beating up spray with its wings.

Like other divers, the red-throated species loses its flight feathers in late summer, and is grounded until new ones grow – though it can still dive for food. It takes to the coast in winter but breeds on small Highland lochs, nesting in shallow water or near the shoreline, and usually laying two dark olive eggs, spotted or blotched blackish-brown. Chicks hatch in about four weeks, swim within 24 hours and fly at around six weeks.

A reedy cooing is the bird's most musical call. Country folk used to think the mewing wail of a courting bird heralded rain, and named it the 'rain goose'.

Location	Behaviour	Sketch
Date		
Time		
Weather	Field marks	
Call		

Black and white neck and back

Wing-beats are slightly slower and shallower than those of red-throated diver.

Downy young, uniform grey and similar to red-throated diver, sometimes ride on back of adult.

SITES GUIDE

The black-throated diver's nest is usually a heap of moss or water plants, on larger lochs than those used by the red-throated diver.

The species may be seen at sites numbers: 2, 13, 44, 54, 56, 65.

Adult in breeding plumage shows striking black and white patterns. Head is more rounded than red-throated diver's. Divers are ungainly on land, as legs are set back for underwater swimming. Sexes are alike. 23–27 in. (58–68 cm).

Present all year; in winter mainly on coasts.

Winter plumage is darker than that of red-throated diver, with sharper demarcation between dark and light areas on head and neck.

Black-throated diver *Gavia arctica*

A big dark bird seen swimming out into a large freshwater loch in Scotland is likely to be a black-throated diver. This species has a definite preference for the bigger stretches of water which its slightly smaller cousin, the red-throated diver, shuns. One of the most haunting sounds of the north-western highlands of Scotland and the outer isles is the wailing cry of the black-throated diver, echoing against the mountains as it asserts ownership of its territory. Its call in flight is a sharp 'kwuk-kwuk-kwuk'.

The bird feeds on fish of all sizes from cod to sprats, and also on shellfish. The eggs normally number two, though one or three are occasionally laid. They are slightly glossy, olive-green or orange-brown in colour, with black speckles and blotches. They hatch after just under a month of incubation.

The chicks return to the nest for their first few nights, but subsequently sleep under the adults' wings, 'riding' on the backs of the swimming birds. The chicks start catching some of their own food within eight to ten weeks of hatching, by which time they are starting to fly. They do not become fully independent until they have left the breeding loch.

Location	Behaviour	Sketch
Date		
Time		
Weather	Field marks	
Call		

Golden tufts

White patch on front of wing, near shoulder, is distinctive. Less white on back of wing than black-necked grebe.

Chestnut neck

Adult in breeding plumage has horn-like golden tufts; neck and flanks are chestnut. Chicks, paler and more striped than young of black-necked grebe, often ride on parent's back. Sexes are alike. 13 in. (33 cm).

Present all year near coasts, but nowhere common.

In winter plumage, cheeks are whiter than those of black-necked grebe, and head shape is flatter.

Slavonian grebe *Podiceps auritus*

Progress has been slow and uncertain for this eye-catching bird since the first breeding pair were seen in Scotland in 1908. They presumably came from Scandinavia or Iceland, the nearest foreign breeding grounds. Even today there are fewer than 60 pairs, concentrated on shallow freshwater lochs in remoter parts of Scotland. They seem more vulnerable than other grebes to human disturbance and still suffer, because of their rarity, from the illegal activities of egg collectors.

After wintering on coastal waters, paired birds return to their breeding grounds and take part in an elaborate ritual of display ceremonies before they mate. Their nests of floating water-weed, sometimes only a few feet apart, are hidden among rocks or under drooping tree branches, and are anchored to plants growing from the lake bottom.

Egg numbers vary widely, but the usual clutch is four or five. The chicks hatch in three to three and a half weeks and quickly leave the nest. Although they can dive well after ten days, they rely on their parents for food almost until the time they can fly, at about two months. Slavonian grebes' main food is water insects, grubs and small fish.

Location	Behaviour	Sketch
Date		
Time		
Weather	Field marks	
Call		

The wings are narrow. The bird takes to the air less frequently than other species of grebe.

Ear-tuft

Black neck and golden ear-tufts identify adult in breeding plumage. Head feathers are raised in a crest in displays. Sexes are alike. 12 in. (30 cm).

Black neck

Steep forehead and slightly upturned point of bill distinguish bird in winter plumage from Slavonian grebe.

Present all year; joined by Continental migrants.

Sites Guide

The black-necked grebe's nest is a pile of water-weed anchored among reeds or sedges in shallow water, and often set in colonies.

The species may be seen at sites numbers: 13, 35, 40 and 49.

Black-necked grebe *Podiceps nigricollis*

Most grebes require extensive areas of open water for successful breeding, but the black-necked grebe is an exception. This attractive little bird, not much bigger than the little grebe, requires pools with a rich growth of water plants both fringing the water and submerged and floating in it; often such pools have very limited open water. Only a few such sites exist in Britain, and this is probably the main reason why the species is scarce in this country. A few central Scottish lochs provide the black-necked grebe's only reliable breeding areas, though elsewhere it may choose a spot for just one season before moving on and sometimes it may take to man-made stretches of water such as reservoirs and sewage farms.

Outside the breeding season the black-necked grebe makes for open waters, including estuaries or sea channels. It is a capable diver and eats small fish, but prefers insects, grubs and other food taken from the surface or from vegetation.

Springtime courtship involves a variety of paired displays, including a water dance similar to that of the great crested grebe, in which two birds rear up breast to breast or side by side. The nest contains three or four eggs, hatched in three weeks.

Location	Behaviour	Sketch
Date		
Time		
Weather	Field marks	
Call		

Wings are held stiffly outstretched as the bird glides low over the sea.

White underparts catch the light as the birds bank. Their long, narrow wings are well adapted for sustained fast gliding.

Birds with dark-coloured heads and underparts are found in Arctic waters.

Grey back

White head

The fulmar's build is bulky, with a heavy bill and thick neck. Sexes are alike. 18¼ in. (47 cm).

Courting pairs cackle and croon. Clumsy on land, they squat on their lower legs.

Present all year; at nest sites in most months.

The fulmar can be identified at close range by prominent tubular nostrils set on top of the bill.

Fulmar *Fulmarus glacialis*

Intruders on the nesting territory of the fulmar meet with an unusually hostile reception. The fulmar brings up a stinking oil, produced from its stomach, and squirts it over the enemy in an accurately aimed jet. Even a young fulmar chick can defend itself in this way.

The fulmar population has increased astonishingly in the last two centuries. Fulmars were first noted in Iceland around 1750, and pairs had settled in the Faeroes by 1820 and in the Shetlands by 1878. By 1970 these few pioneers had increased to more than 300,000 pairs around the coasts of Britain and Ireland. This increase in population is the more remarkable in that the birds do not breed until they are six or more years old – and even then lay only one egg a year. A factor that may have helped them is the vast expansion of fishing, the fish offal thrown overboard providing large quantities of food for seabirds.

A single egg is laid in any convenient depression on a cliff ledge or offshore rock pillar. Incubation takes about 50 days, the parents sharing the task in shifts. During the seven weeks before the hatched chick can fly, they give it food regurgitated from their own stomachs.

Location	Behaviour	Sketch
Date		
Time		
Weather	Field marks	
Call		

Black crown

White chin, throat

A bird with sharply contrasting plumage: its upper parts are black, its underparts white or greyish-white. Sexes are alike. 14 in. (36 cm).

Birds assemble in huge flocks near their nesting colonies at dusk.

Flight alternates between gliding and rapid flapping, both with stiff wings.

Feb.–Oct. visitor, breeding on west coast islands.

A skilful and buoyant swimmer, the bird keeps its head and tail well up.

The chick has dense down; it does not leave its burrow until it flies, at about ten weeks old.

Sites Guide

Manx shearwaters nest in burrows on the cliff tops of islands, and occasionally of the mainland. Burrows are close and often collapse.

The species may be seen at sites numbers: 1, 9, 12, 19, 23, 44, 47, 52, 58, 62, 64.

Manx shearwater *Puffinus puffinus*

After an absence of 150 years, this remarkable bird has returned in strength to breed on the Isle of Man from which its name is derived. There are thriving colonies on other islands off Britain's western coast. Manx shearwaters come to land only to breed; when the breeding season is over many cross the Atlantic to spend the winter at sea off the coast of South America.

Manx shearwaters fly with powerful wing beats, interspersed with long glides in which they skim the surface of the water, appearing even to 'shear' the waves. The bird is one of nature's most brilliant navigators. One bird from the Welsh island of Skokholm was taken to Massachusetts, over 3,000 miles across the North Atlantic and outside its normal range. It was rêleased there, and took only 12 days to return to its chick.

Icelandic sagas of the early 11th century refer to the eerie, unnerving din that these birds set up as the adults come back to their nests from feeding at sea, particularly in the hour before midnight. The Manx shearwater builds its nest in a burrow, and the parents take turns to incubate the single egg. About 60 days after hatching, the chicks are deserted, and a week or ten days later they make their way to the sea.

Location	Behaviour	Sketch
Date		
Time		
Weather	Field marks	
Call		

Seen from below in flight, white patches under wings are conspicuous. Tail is square and black.

Pale wing-bar

White rump

Storm petrel is sooty black, except for white rump and pale wing-bar. Sexes are alike. 6 in. (15 cm).

Leach's petrel

Wilson's petrel

Two rarer petrels

Leach's petrel (*Oceanodroma leucorrhoa*) is black-ish-brown with a white rump and a forked tail. The inner wing shows a paler brown diagonal band on top. Under-wings are dark. Even rarer is Wilson's petrel (*Oceanites oceanicus*), which can be distinguished by its long legs and yellow-webbed feet that may extend beyond the tail; the tail is not forked.

Storm petrel *Hydrobates pelagicus*

When the storm or stormy petrel followed the wake of a vessel, it was believed to forecast the coming of a storm. In fact the bird probably follows ships in order to feed on the marine life brought to the surface in the disturbance of their passage. The name 'petrel' is said to be a diminutive of Peter: when feeding, the bird flits and hovers just above the water, often with feet pattering on the surface, appearing to 'walk on the water' as St Peter did in the Bible story. The storm petrel is also called Mother Carey's chicken, a name that may be a corruption of *Mater Cara*, 'Dear Mother', the name formerly given by sailors in the eastern Mediterranean to the Virgin Mary.

The storm petrel spends its entire life on the open sea except when breeding, when it comes ashore at night to remote and lonely islands off the western shores of the British Isles. Colonies may vary in size from a few pairs to many thousands. A single, dull white egg is laid. The chick is at first covered thickly in greyish-brown down, but grows a second plumage of darker down before the flight feathers develop.

The larger Leach's petrel does not customarily follow ships, but the very similar Wilson's petrel has this habit.

Location	Behaviour	Sketch
Date		
Time		
Weather	Field marks	
Call		

Immature,
second year,
in flight.

Adult gannet's plumage is white, except for a buff head and nape and black wingtips. Winter and summer plumages are similar. Legs are black; the large, pointed bill turns down at the tip. The bird has a wing-span of up to 6 ft (1·8 m). Sexes are alike. 36 in. (90 cm).

Present all year; most common in north and west.

Gannet *Sula bassana*

When crowds of gannets nest in an offshore colony, or gannetry, they are at their most aggressive. The nests are evenly spaced on sloping rocks or wide ledges, and the birds keep just out of pecking distance of each other. But if an adult lands in the wrong place, or a chick strays from its nest, the offender is mercilessly attacked and is sometimes pecked to death.

A gannetry may contain as many as 60,000 pairs of birds. The air above such a colony is usually full of birds. Some of them hang on motionless wings in the strong updraught at the side of a rock, while others fly in from fishing trips on 6 ft (1·8 m) wing-spans. Their calls are loud, bark-like 'urrahs' and 'aarrhs', and the collective sound of many thousands of gannets in a large colony is almost deafening.

The nests consist of large heaps of seaweed and other plants, and materials such as feathers. The clutch is nearly always a single egg; two-egg clutches are very rare. The egg is rather elongated with an irregular chalky coating, so thin in places that the pale blue shell can be seen through it. The parents take turns at incubation, for which they use their overlapping, webbed feet. The chick hatches after 43–45 days.

Location	Behaviour	Sketch
Date		
Time		
Weather	Field marks	
Call		

Non-breeding plumage lacks the white thigh-patch.

Nestling has thick black down and a bare face.

White cheeks

Upright, spread-wing stance is a characteristic posture.

Thigh-patch

Adult in breeding plumage is identified by white cheeks and chin and white patch on thigh. Sexes are alike. 36 in. (90 cm).

Present all year on coasts, and frequently inland.

Immature bird is brownish, but paler underparts distinguish it from an immature shag. Flight is goose-like, with head held up.

Bird swims low in water with head held high and tilted upwards.

Sites Guide

Cormorants breed in close colonies, building their nests mainly of twigs and seaweed. Cliff ledges are favourite sites.

The species may be seen at sites numbers: 1, 4-6, 10-14, 19-21, 23, 41, 44, 52.

Cormorant *Phalacrocorax carbo*

Fishermen have tended to persecute the cormorant in the belief, perhaps unfair, that its combination of fishing skill and large appetite depleted stocks – especially in rivers, where it was said to favour trout, young salmon and eels. Researches show, however, that cormorants seem to favour flat fish and eels, taking only a small proportion of marketable fish. Enterprising Japanese and Chinese make use of the cormorant's expertise by training one species to dive and catch fish for them.

Cormorants are members of the pelican family, with all four toes on each foot webbed, which aids them in swimming and pursuing fish under water. Emerging from the waves, they are often seen standing on a rock or jetty with wings outstretched, apparently drying them; but why a bird that spends so much time in the sea should not have evolved efficient waterproofing like other marine birds remains a mystery.

Some cormorant colonies have hundreds, or even thousands, of birds. They build large nests on cliff tops and rocky islets, sometimes by rivers and lakes – even in trees. Three or four eggs are laid; the chicks hatch in about a month, and are fed once a day by each parent with regurgitated food.

Location	Behaviour	Sketch
Date		
Time		
Weather	Field marks	
Call		

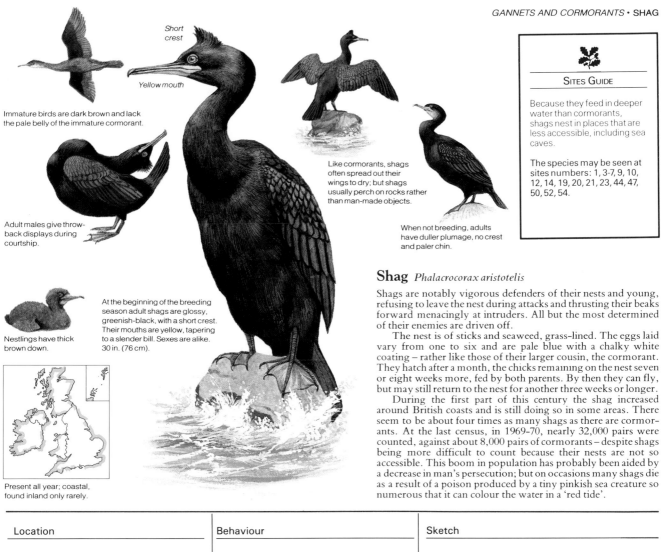

Short crest

Yellow mouth

Immature birds are dark brown and lack the pale belly of the immature cormorant.

Adult males give throw-back displays during courtship.

Nestlings have thick brown down.

At the beginning of the breeding season adult shags are glossy, greenish-black, with a short crest. Their mouths are yellow, tapering to a slender bill. Sexes are alike. 30 in. (76 cm).

Present all year; coastal, found inland only rarely.

Like cormorants, shags often spread out their wings to dry; but shags usually perch on rocks rather than man-made objects.

When not breeding, adults have duller plumage, no crest and paler chin.

Sites Guide

Because they feed in deeper water than cormorants, shags nest in places that are less accessible, including sea caves.

The species may be seen at sites numbers: 1, 3-7, 9, 10, 12, 14, 19, 20, 21, 23, 44, 47, 50, 52, 54.

Shag *Phalacrocorax aristotelis*

Shags are notably vigorous defenders of their nests and young, refusing to leave the nest during attacks and thrusting their beaks forward menacingly at intruders. All but the most determined of their enemies are driven off.

The nest is of sticks and seaweed, grass-lined. The eggs laid vary from one to six and are pale blue with a chalky white coating – rather like those of their larger cousin, the cormorant. They hatch after a month, the chicks remaining on the nest seven or eight weeks more, fed by both parents. By then they can fly, but may still return to the nest for another three weeks or longer.

During the first part of this century the shag increased around British coasts and is still doing so in some areas. There seem to be about four times as many shags as there are cormorants. At the last census, in 1969-70, nearly 32,000 pairs were counted, against about 8,000 pairs of cormorants – despite shags being more difficult to count because their nests are not so accessible. This boom in population has probably been aided by a decrease in man's persecution; but on occasions many shags die as a result of a poison produced by a tiny pinkish sea creature so numerous that it can colour the water in a 'red tide'.

Location	Behaviour	Sketch
Date		
Time		
Weather	Field marks	
Call		

Orange bill

Curved neck

Flight is powerful, with outstretched neck. When wings are beating, flight feathers produce loud, throbbing hum.

Cygnets (chicks) are pale grey above and white below; about six to a brood.

Curved neck which distinguishes adult mute swan is apparent even when swan rears out of water to repel an intruder. Male, or cob, has larger knob at base of orange bill than female. 60 in. (152 cm).

Present all year; nests all over Britain except far north.

Threat display of adult male defending family consists of drawing back and folding wings above back while surging forward in water. Female often carries young on back.

Mute swan *Cygnus olor*

This graceful bird's nature belies its placid, decorative appearance: it is extremely quarrelsome, and bullies smaller species. In the breeding season the male stakes out a large area of water and defends this territory aggressively against all-comers. The bird's name, too, is deceptive, for although quieter than Britain's two wild swans, the whooper and Bewick's, it hisses and snorts when angry, and may trumpet feebly.

All mute swans on the River Thames belong either to the Crown or to one of two London livery companies: the Vintners' Company and the Dyers' Company. In the third week of July, cygnets as far upstream as Henley-on-Thames are rounded up when they are flightless during the moult. Those that are owned by the livery companies are marked by having their bills notched; those left unmarked belong to the Crown. This 'swan-upping' ceremony dates back to the Middle Ages, when swans were highly valued as a table delicacy.

The nest is an enormous mound of water plants up to 13 ft (4 m) across and 30 in. (76 cm) high. Normally four to seven eggs are laid, and they are incubated for 34–38 days, mainly by the female, or pen. The young fly in four and a half months.

Location	Behaviour	Sketch
Date		
Time		
Weather	Field marks	
Call		

Brent geese fly in long wavering lines, usually low above water or ground.

In flight, birds are identified by dark plumage and white stern.

Black head and neck

White neck-patch

Pale-bellied race has whitish underparts.

Dark-bellied race from Russia has slate-grey underparts.

Young goose has white edges to the wing coverts, and lacks white neck-patch.

A dark, black and grey goose with a noticeable white stern. It is only slightly larger than the mallard. Adult has a black head, neck and breast with a small white patch on the neck, and dark grey-brown back. The bill is short and the head narrow. Sexes are alike. 22–24 in. (55–60 cm).

Oct.–Apr. visitor, spreading inland to feed.

Sites Guide

Excellent swimmers, Brent geese spend much of their time afloat, feeding on eel-grass and seaweed.

The species may be seen at sites numbers: 12-15, 17, 18, 30, 31, 45, 57, 65.

Brent goose *Branta bernicla*

Small, dark Brent geese, winter visitors to Britain from the Arctic tundra, all but died out in the 1930s. One reason for this decline was that disease struck their main winter food plant, the eel-grass that grows on tidal flats and in estuaries around the North Sea. The number dropped by three-quarters, but under strict protection the species is recovering. Flocks, flying low in straggly but disciplined formation or roosting on the water, are no longer a rare sight off the east and south coasts. The eel-grass is apparently recovering too, but the Brent goose now also raids winter cereals to supplement its diet.

Two races of Brent geese winter in England. Dark-bellied geese from Arctic Russia visit the south-east and pale-bellied Brents from Spitzbergen and Franz Josef Land arrive in north-east England and Denmark, while others of the same race, from Greenland and even Canada, pass the winter in Ireland.

When feeding at sea, Brent geese bob like ducks with their white sterns in the air. In the tundra, the geese begin nesting before the ice and snow have melted. They lay three to five eggs which hatch in three and a half weeks, and within three months the young birds must be ready to fly south.

Location	Behaviour	Sketch
Date		
Time		
Weather	Field marks	
Call		

Flocks of barnacle geese often fly in irregular, ragged packs with a chain stringing out behind – but never in regular formation. Stragglers are sometimes found in flocks of grey geese.

White face and light belly of adult contrast strikingly with other plumage in flight.

White face

Black neck

A white face contrasting with black crown, neck and breast make the adult barnacle goose unmistakable. Upper parts are grey with white-edged black bars. Sexes are alike. 23–27 in. (58–68 cm).

Mating displays include a characteristic wing-flicking action as paired birds rush about, calling loudly.

Juvenile bird has duller head and neck plumage than adult.

Oct.–Apr. visitor, mainly to west Scotland, Ireland.

Barnacle goose *Branta leucopsis*

In the air or on the ground, family groups of barnacle geese bicker continually with a noise like yapping, yelping small dogs. Rarely silent for long, they produce the loudest clamour of all when taking flight. Coastal grass that is periodically flooded by high tides is their favourite food, but if none is available they graze on pastureland – leading to occasional complaints from farmers that they foul it with their droppings.

Family bonds are strong: although goslings can soon look after themselves, they stay with their parents until the next breeding season. For their annual migrations, family groups join together in larger travelling parties.

Wintering flocks come to the British Isles from two separate homelands, and they stay apart. Those that visit the Solway Firth area breed on the Arctic island of Spitsbergen. Birds seen in western Scotland and Ireland are from Greenland. Before the Arctic was explored and the nesting grounds found, people thought that the birds grew on trees. They also believed that the barnacles seen on floating timber were the embryos of the birds, and so came to apply the same name to both the bird and the crustacean.

Location	Behaviour	Sketch
Date		
Time		
Weather	Field marks	
Call		

Birds fly with slow wing-beats and may form lines or wedges. Ducks utter an 'ak-ak-ak' call, drakes a soft whistle.

Dark green head

Red bill

Juveniles have much white about the head and underparts. They are generally duller in colour than adults, with brownish-grey upper parts.

Rusty breast-band

Adult female in duller 'eclipse' plumage. It patters on the mud with its feet to bring prey to the surface.

Adult male in breeding plumage. It has a bright red bill, very dark green head, and white body with rust-coloured breast-band. 24 in. (60 cm).

The head-up 'salute' is used between birds that have paired to show they intend to take flight.

Present all year; coastal, but increasing inland.

The female is distinguished by the lack of a bill knob. Ducklings are white with broad, deep brown stripes.

Shelduck *Tadorna tadorna*

These colourful waterfowl leave Britain each summer, usually in July, for the annual 'moult migration' that follows the breeding season. Thousands gather in the tidal estuaries of the Heligoland Bight off the north German coast, where they become flightless for three to four weeks while their entire plumage is renewed. They return in autumn.

After three to six months, the new, duller 'eclipse' plumage gives way to the handsome breeding plumage. The nest is made by the female and sparsely lined with grass and insulated with down and feathers from the bird's own breast. It is often placed 8–10 ft (2·5–3 m) down a rabbit burrow in sand-dunes, or in a similar hole. The duck lays a single clutch of 8–15 creamy-white eggs, usually in early May, and she does all the sitting while the drake remains near by. The ducklings, which hatch in just under a month, are led to the nearest water by one or both parents. They can dive expertly if threatened, and are independent after about two months. Broods tend to join up in large crèches.

A favourite food of the shelduck is the small marine snail called *hydrobia*. They also eat small shellfish, insects, fish, worms and some vegetable matter.

Location	Behaviour	Sketch
Date		
Time		
Weather	Field marks	
Call		

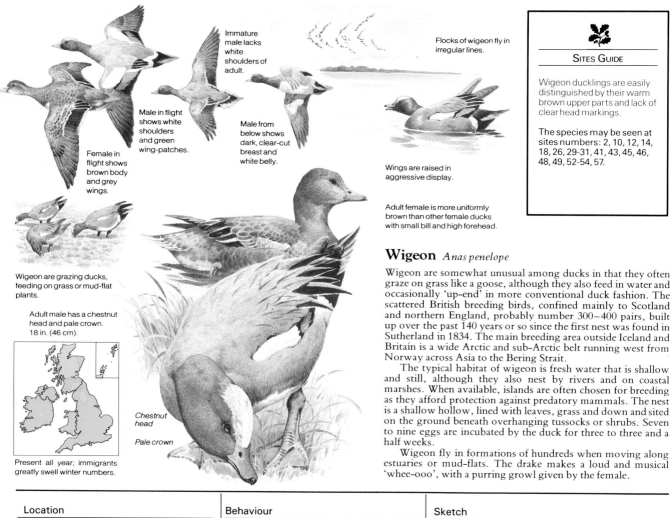

Immature male lacks white shoulders of adult.

Flocks of wigeon fly in irregular lines.

Male in flight shows white shoulders and green wing-patches.

Male from below shows dark, clear-cut breast and white belly.

Female in flight shows brown body and grey wings.

Wings are raised in aggressive display.

Adult female is more uniformly brown than other female ducks with small bill and high forehead.

Wigeon are grazing ducks, feeding on grass or mud-flat plants.

Adult male has a chestnut head and pale crown. 18 in. (46 cm).

Chestnut head

Pale crown

Present all year; immigrants greatly swell winter numbers.

SITES GUIDE

Wigeon ducklings are easily distinguished by their warm brown upper parts and lack of clear head markings.

The species may be seen at sites numbers: 2, 10, 12, 14, 18, 26, 29-31, 41, 43, 45, 46, 48, 49, 52-54, 57.

Wigeon *Anas penelope*

Wigeon are somewhat unusual among ducks in that they often graze on grass like a goose, although they also feed in water and occasionally 'up-end' in more conventional duck fashion. The scattered British breeding birds, confined mainly to Scotland and northern England, probably number 300–400 pairs, built up over the past 140 years or so since the first nest was found in Sutherland in 1834. The main breeding area outside Iceland and Britain is a wide Arctic and sub-Arctic belt running west from Norway across Asia to the Bering Strait.

The typical habitat of wigeon is fresh water that is shallow and still, although they also nest by rivers and on coastal marshes. When available, islands are often chosen for breeding as they afford protection against predatory mammals. The nest is a shallow hollow, lined with leaves, grass and down and sited on the ground beneath overhanging tussocks or shrubs. Seven to nine eggs are incubated by the duck for three to three and a half weeks.

Wigeon fly in formations of hundreds when moving along estuaries or mud-flats. The drake makes a loud and musical 'whee-ooo', with a purring growl given by the female.

Location	Behaviour	Sketch
Date		
Time		
Weather	Field marks	
Call		

Both sexes show a broad white wing-bar in flight.

Male

Female

Grey back

Male has blackish head and breast, white underparts and grey bill like the tufted duck, but is distinguished by pale grey back and lack of crest. 19 in. (48 cm).

Present all year; mainly found on estuaries.

Female has brown head and upper parts. A large white patch at base of bill distinguishes it from the tufted duck. Ducklings are tended by the female and led to water almost as soon as their down is dry.

Scaup feed at sea, often in dense flocks.

Sand-banks serve as resting places. Scaup are rarely seen inland.

SITES GUIDE

At close range the head of the male scaup has a green gloss, as distinct from the brown head of the female.

The species may be seen at sites numbers: 10, 43, 45, 46, 53.

Scaup *Aythya marila*

This bird's odd name was thought by the ornithologist George Montagu (1751–1815) to be derived from its habit of feeding on broken shells, called scaup. Its diet is largely made up of molluscs, especially mussels; it also eats crustaceans such as crabs, and various insects and worms.

Species that breed very rarely in Britain are protected by law, and the scaup, or scaup-duck as it used to be known, is one of these. In the breeding season scaup frequent inland waters such as lakes and rivers, but in winter they mostly take to the sea, often gathering in large feeding flocks off the coasts.

In its courtship display the male swims towards the female with head stretched up and bill pointing steeply upwards. It also displays with a quick stretching-up of the head and a cooing call. Scaup often breed in spread-out colonies on islands in lakes. The nest is a scrape or hollow, frequently in an open situation but occasionally protected by a tussock of grass. It is lined with vegetation and insulated with down from the female's breast. The eggs, laid from late May onwards, usually number 6–12 or sometimes more. They take three to four weeks to hatch, and the chicks become independent at about six weeks old.

Location	Behaviour	Sketch
Date		
Time		
Weather	Field marks	
Call		

Male

Male in flight
shows black rump,
tail and flight
feathers, with
rest of body white.
Female is mainly
brown.

Female

Bill-tossing and neck-
jerking are features of the
male's courtship display.

Adult female is mottled
brown and has a low,
sloping head with the bill
extending back to the
forehead.

Black cap

Male, eclipse
phase

Adult male has black cap and
belly, the rest of its plumage
appearing white; at close quarters
the breast is pinkish and the nape
of the neck green. When flight
feathers moult, other plumage
darkens in a less conspicuous
'eclipse' phase. 23 in. (58 cm).

Black
belly

Present all year on north
coasts, local visitor in south.

Eider *Somateria mollissima*

Bedding manufacturers have found no better insulating material
for the traditional eiderdown than the soft breast down of the
female eider, which she grows especially to protect the clutch of
eggs in the nest. Duck-down farmers remove it in carefully
limited quantities for commercial use.

The voice of the drake eider is a cooing 'ooo-ooo-ooo', with
the middle syllable slightly higher than the rest in pitch. The
eider often breeds in colonies on offshore islands, on the coast,
or on the shores of lakes and rivers, generally in rather exposed
sites. Eiders are thoroughly at home in rough seas, swimming
easily through the surf round rocky coasts and islets while
diving for molluscs.

The breeding season begins early in April in northern
England, and some six weeks later in northern Scotland. One
clutch of three to ten eggs is produced each year. The female,
crouching close to the ground, incubates her eggs for long,
unbroken spells over a period of about a month. The ducklings,
mainly blackish-brown in colour, are led down to the water
soon after hatching. They are able to look after themselves at
about 9–11 weeks old.

Location	Behaviour	Sketch
Date		
Time		
Weather	Field marks	
Call		

Female, winter

Male, winter

Both sexes are recognised in flight by the absence of bars on their wings and by their unusual flying action, with shallow wing upstrokes but deep downstrokes.

Male, winter

Male, winter

Adult male in winter plumage. Males are distinguished at all times by their long tail; only the pintail, differently marked, has one like it. The female has dark cheek-patches. Male 21 in. (53 cm); female 16 in. (40 cm).

The male moults gradually throughout the year; by midsummer its head and neck are dark but the face remains white.

Long tail

Courtship features head-tossing and 'rear end' displays.

Sept.–Apr. visitor, but has bred in Scotland.

SITES GUIDE

These ducks usually keep well out to sea and leave in May for breeding grounds in northern Scandinavia.

The species may be seen at sites numbers: 2, 10, 26, 30, 45, 49, 53.

Long-tailed duck *Clangula hyemalis*

The voice of the male long-tailed duck is extraordinary among ducks for its melodious, resonant and far-carrying quality. The variety of its calls, too, is remarkable: the calls of a displaying flock have been likened by some ornithologists to the sound of distant bagpipes.

The period from the end of September to the end of October sees the arrival in British waters of the wintering population of long-tailed ducks from their northern breeding grounds. The nest, a mere scrape in the ground sparsely lined with plant material and down, is usually sited in thick vegetation not far from water; occasionally it is in a rock crevice. The duck incubates its six to nine olive-buff eggs for about three and a half weeks. The ducklings' down is brown tipped with gold above and greyish-white below. Occasionally several broods may join together in a *crèche* – a phenomenon found in several species of waterfowl, for example eider and shelduck. The young become independent after about five weeks.

This bird's food consists predominantly of animal life such as molluscs and crustaceans, which it gathers by diving, but it also enjoys seeds, leaves and other vegetable matter.

Location	Behaviour	Sketch
Date		
Time		
Weather	Field marks	
Call		

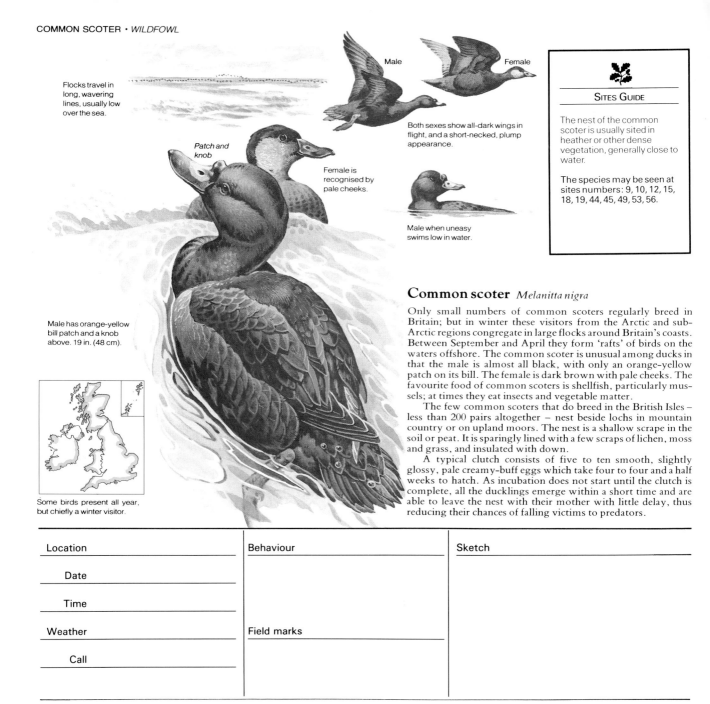

Flocks travel in long, wavering lines, usually low over the sea.

Male

Female

Both sexes show all-dark wings in flight, and a short-necked, plump appearance.

Patch and knob

Female is recognised by pale cheeks.

Male when uneasy swims low in water.

Male has orange-yellow bill patch and a knob above. 19 in. (48 cm).

Some birds present all year, but chiefly a winter visitor.

SITES GUIDE

The nest of the common scoter is usually sited in heather or other dense vegetation, generally close to water.

The species may be seen at sites numbers: 9, 10, 12, 15, 18, 19, 44, 45, 49, 53, 56.

Common scoter *Melanitta nigra*

Only small numbers of common scoters regularly breed in Britain; but in winter these visitors from the Arctic and sub-Arctic regions congregate in large flocks around Britain's coasts. Between September and April they form 'rafts' of birds on the waters offshore. The common scoter is unusual among ducks in that the male is almost all black, with only an orange-yellow patch on its bill. The female is dark brown with pale cheeks. The favourite food of common scoters is shellfish, particularly mussels; at times they eat insects and vegetable matter.

The few common scoters that do breed in the British Isles – less than 200 pairs altogether – nest beside lochs in mountain country or on upland moors. The nest is a shallow scrape in the soil or peat. It is sparingly lined with a few scraps of lichen, moss and grass, and insulated with down.

A typical clutch consists of five to ten smooth, slightly glossy, pale creamy-buff eggs which take four to four and a half weeks to hatch. As incubation does not start until the clutch is complete, all the ducklings emerge within a short time and are able to leave the nest with their mother with little delay, thus reducing their chances of falling victims to predators.

Location	Behaviour	Sketch
Date		
Time		
Weather	Field marks	
Call		

Male

Female

Flight is fast and direct, with neck and body outstretched to produce a long, narrow shape. White wing-patch is more extensive on male.

Double crest

Fishing birds often swim with head under water before submerging totally to dive on prey.

Red-brown breast

During its moult the male resembles the female, but back is darker and forewing whiter.

Adult female in breeding plumage has shorter crest than the male. The brown colouring of the head merges into neck and breast.

Present all year; mainly on estuaries in winter.

Downy young are generally dark above and pale below, with white spots on their wings and backs.

Adult male has dark green head and reddish-brown breast and neck. Double crest and darker colouring distinguish it from goosander. 23 in. (58 cm).

Red-breasted merganser *Mergus serrator*

These ducks have a bad reputation among trout and salmon fishermen because of their taste for the young of the two fish. Defenders of the red-breasted merganser argue, however, that they also eat many non–game species, including eels, perch and pike which compete with or prey on the eggs or the young of salmon and trout.

The red-breasted merganser and the goosander are the only two species of sawbill duck that breed in the British Isles. They have finely serrated cutting edges to their bills that enable them to grasp slippery fish. The red-breasted merganser has a long history of residence in Scotland and Ireland. Since about 1950, however, in spite of some persecution, birds have spread into England, breeding as far south as Derbyshire, and also into Wales.

The nest is a shallow depression in the ground lined with grass, leaves and down. Thick vegetation usually makes it hard to find. From late April to early July the female lays and incubates eight to ten pale buff eggs that take a month to hatch. When the female leaves the nest, she camouflages the eggs with down. The ducklings can fly about two months after hatching.

Location	Behaviour	Sketch
Date		
Time		
Weather	Field marks	
Call		

Adult male is pale grey above and white below. It is larger and bulkier than Montagu's harrier. 17 in. (43 cm).

Dark wingtips

Male in flight shows white rump and dark wingtips.

White rump

Adult female is brown above and brown-and-white streaked below, with black bars on its wings. It is larger than the male. 20 in. (50 cm).

Female is called from nest by male to catch prey that he drops to her; she rolls over as she catches it.

Adult female in flight shows white rump and barred tail.

Present all year; breeding range spreading south.

SITES GUIDE

The female hen harrier builds a nest of grass, heather and bracken on the ground, usually among moorland heather.

The species may be seen at sites numbers: 11-13, 15, 17, 18, 24, 27, 40, 43, 46, 48.

Hen harrier *Circus cyaneus*

Pouncing from a low-level hunting glide, this moorland marauder is far from particular about its prey. Almost any creature up to the size of a hare or a duck is fair game for its powerful talons. Small mammals and birds, including the chicks of other birds of prey, make up most of the hen harrier's diet, but it also eats lizards, snakes, frogs, beetles and the eggs of ground-nesting birds.

Centuries ago, when the bird was more widespread, it preyed on domestic poultry and so obtained its name; today, however, it is considered to be little threat to the farmyard hen. Hen harriers became very rare in the early part of this century, vanishing entirely from mainland Britain by about 1940 and surviving only in the Orkneys and Outer Hebrides. Since all Britain's hawks gained the protection of the law, however, hen harriers have shown a particularly large population increase.

Breeding areas of the hen harrier are now spreading back through England, Wales and Ireland, and birds are nesting in birch and willow scrub, young fir plantations and even among crops, as well as in their traditional moor and marsh areas. Chicks hatch in about five weeks and fly at five weeks old.

Location	Behaviour	Sketch
Date		
Time		
Weather	Field marks	
Call		

Perching buzzard has an upright stance and shows a heavy, rounded build.

In gliding, wings are held flat with primary feathers turned back and pointed.

Wings are held forward and raised when soaring, with primary feathers turned up and tail widely spread.

Legs are unfeathered, unlike those of the visiting rough-legged buzzard.

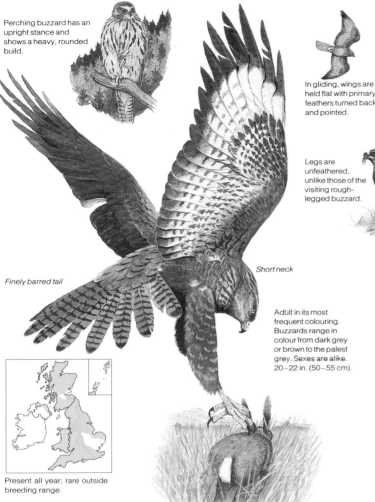

Finely barred tail

Short neck

Adult in its most frequent colouring. Buzzards range in colour from dark grey or brown to the palest grey. Sexes are alike. 20–22 in. (50–55 cm).

Present all year; rare outside breeding range.

SITES GUIDE

Buzzards favour trees and cliff ledges for nesting. The bulky nest is built of sticks and 'decorated' with greenery.

The species may be seen at sites numbers: 3, 8, 11, 20-25, 27, 28, 35, 36, 38, 40-42, 48, 51-53.

Buzzard *Buteo buteo*

A familiar sound in hilly country in western or northern Britain is the mewing 'kiew' of a buzzard as it sails apparently without effort over a neighbouring hillside, circling in the updraught from the hill or in a rising thermal of hot air. The keen-sighted bird meanwhile scans the ground below for prey. Small mammals are its favourite food, in particular rabbits – so much so that the number of buzzards declined dramatically after myxomatosis almost wiped out Britain's rabbit population in the mid-1950s.

Buzzards prefer open hillsides and wooded valleys like those of South Wales, the Lake District and western Scotland; they are fewer in bare, mountainous regions and moorland. They build large nests of sticks or heather stalks and line them with finer twigs, bracken, grass, moss or seaweed.

The handsome eggs have a white or bluish-white shell decorated with brown spots or blotches. They take about a month to hatch, and since the eggs are laid at intervals of three or four days the young are of variable age. Young birds often die of starvation when food is short, but despite this, buzzards remain the most common of Britain's larger birds of prey.

Location	Behaviour	Sketch
Date		
Time		
Weather	Field marks	
Call		

Display flights consist of alternate swoops and glides.

Gold head

Adults in flight show dark underparts.

Immature birds in flight show white patches on wings and tail when seen from below.

Prey as heavy as a fox can be lifted with a downhill take-off.

Golden eagles sometimes hunt in pairs, especially in winter.

Present all year; rarely occurs beyond breeding range.

Adults are distinguishable from other birds of prey by their great size and flat profile of head and bill. Head has a golden tinge; body and wings are darker. Male 30–35 in. (76–89 cm); female about 35 in. (89 cm).

Golden eagle *Aquila chrysaetos*

An observer has only to glimpse a golden eagle once to realise why it is traditionally regarded in Britain as the king of birds. In flight, it gives an impression of unequalled power and control, with long, broad wings stretched out and wingtip feathers spread as though feeling for the currents of rising air which will bear it up to the Scottish mountain-tops that are its stronghold. The sight is likely to be rare, for each pair of eagles needs a massive 3,000 acre territory.

In close-up the golden eagle presents a magnificent spectacle: it is a large, powerfully built bird with lethal talons. The large, piercing eyes protected from the sun's glare by prominent brows, and the hooked bill – which has given the adjective 'aquiline' to human noses – lend the bird an expression of nobility, set off by its golden nape plumes.

Golden eagles can kill prey up to the size of a fox, but in most areas blue hares, ptarmigan and red grouse probably provide most of their food. Carrion, too, is eaten. The nests are bulky structures of sticks, heather and bracken lined with grass or wood-rushes. Two eggs are usually laid, but only one eaglet normally survives.

Location	Behaviour	Sketch
Date		
Time		
Weather	Field marks	
Call		

The nest, usually on top of a pine tree, is added to each year.

Young birds have paler-edged feathers on their upper parts, but are white below like adults.

Rare Apr.–Oct. visitor; may be seen on passage.

Both sexes have a white, slightly crested head and dark eye-streak. Breasts are dark speckled and underparts white. 20–23 in. (50–58 cm).

Spiny-scaled toes give grip on slippery fish.

Dark speckles

In flight the wings are sharply angled at the wrist joint.

An adult hovers about 100 ft (30 m) above water, then plunges onto its prey.

Sites Guide

An adult osprey can be seen carrying fish weighing up to about 4½lb (2kg). It is also known as a fish hawk.

The species may be seen at sites numbers: 13, 31, 35 and 40.

Osprey *Pandion haliaetus*

An osprey making a kill is a spectacular sight. Fish make up the bulk of its diet, and a hunting bird flies over the water at a considerable height, with alternate spells of flapping and gliding, until it spots a large fish near the surface. It pauses in mid-flight, sometimes hovers momentarily, then turns with half-closed wings and plummets to the water, entering feet first with a large splash and often completely submerging for a moment or two. On surfacing after a successful dive with a fish in its talons, it shakes its plumage violently to remove the water, then carries the fish, often a trout or a pike, back to its nest.

An outstanding success story of recent times was the return of the osprey to its former breeding areas in Scotland. Driven out partly because it competed with anglers for trout, the bird was absent for 50 years. Then, after four years in which they visited but did not breed, one pair raised young in 1959; under constant protection, numbers have built up steadily ever since.

The osprey's large nest, built of sticks, is used for season after season. The eggs are white, with blotches of chocolate or reddish-brown, and are incubated mainly by the hen. Eight or nine weeks may elapse before the young can fly.

Location		Behaviour		Sketch	
Date					
Time					
Weather		Field marks			
Call					

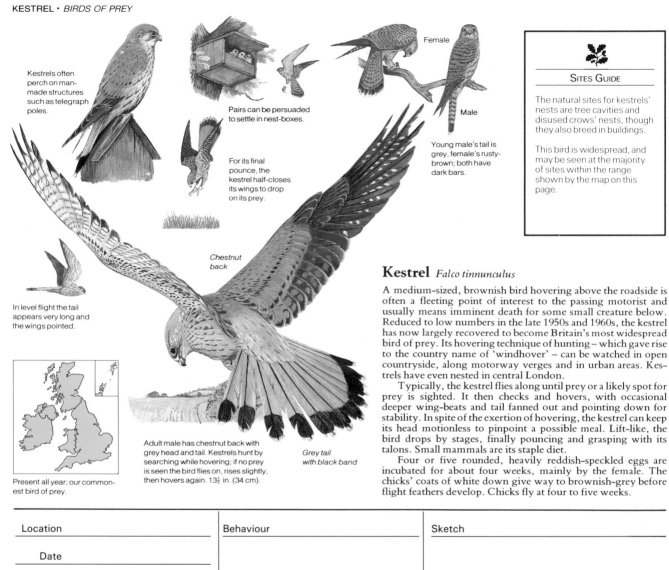

Kestrels often perch on man-made structures such as telegraph poles.

Pairs can be persuaded to settle in nest-boxes.

For its final pounce, the kestrel half-closes its wings to drop on its prey.

Female

Male

Young male's tail is grey, female's rusty-brown; both have dark bars.

Chestnut back

In level flight the tail appears very long and the wings pointed.

Adult male has chestnut back with grey head and tail. Kestrels hunt by searching while hovering; if no prey is seen the bird flies on, rises slightly, then hovers again. 13½ in. (34 cm).

Grey tail with black band

Present all year; our commonest bird of prey.

Sites Guide

The natural sites for kestrels' nests are tree cavities and disused crows' nests, though they also breed in buildings.

This bird is widespread, and may be seen at the majority of sites within the range shown by the map on this page.

Kestrel *Falco tinnunculus*

A medium–sized, brownish bird hovering above the roadside is often a fleeting point of interest to the passing motorist and usually means imminent death for some small creature below. Reduced to low numbers in the late 1950s and 1960s, the kestrel has now largely recovered to become Britain's most widespread bird of prey. Its hovering technique of hunting – which gave rise to the country name of 'windhover' – can be watched in open countryside, along motorway verges and in urban areas. Kestrels have even nested in central London.

Typically, the kestrel flies along until prey or a likely spot for prey is sighted. It then checks and hovers, with occasional deeper wing-beats and tail fanned out and pointing down for stability. In spite of the exertion of hovering, the kestrel can keep its head motionless to pinpoint a possible meal. Lift-like, the bird drops by stages, finally pouncing and grasping with its talons. Small mammals are its staple diet.

Four or five rounded, heavily reddish-speckled eggs are incubated for about four weeks, mainly by the female. The chicks' coats of white down give way to brownish-grey before flight feathers develop. Chicks fly at four to five weeks.

Location	Behaviour	Sketch
Date		
Time		
Weather	Field marks	
Call		

Female and young of both sexes look brown from above when in flight.

Blue-grey upper parts

Adult male has blue-grey upper parts and black tail band. When perched, merlins appear more compact than other falcons. 10½–13 in. (27–33 cm).

Black tail band

In winter, merlins may move to low ground such as marshland to hunt.

The erratic flight is punctuated by short glides. The tail appears shorter than that of the kestrel.

Early in the breeding season, males fly between low perches calling to females.

The low-flying merlin often takes small birds in level flight; but sometimes the quarry escapes by going to ground under a bush or other vegetation.

Present all year; some birds migrate from Iceland.

Merlin *Falco columbarius*

Flying low, fast and level, with quick, shallow wing-beats, the male merlin, little bigger than a mistle thrush, quarters the heather-clad moors of northern and western Britain in search of its prey – mainly small birds, but sometimes insects, lizards and mice. On sighting its prey, the merlin rises above it, then drops to sink its talons into its victim. The merlin carries its prey off to a so-called 'plucking-post' – a rock outcrop, fence or drystone wall where the bird plucks its prey before presenting it to its mate, who takes it back to the nest.

In the 60 days or so it takes merlins to hatch and learn to fly, the male bird hunts for mate and family. Then, while the offspring are maturing – a process that takes a further six weeks – the female joins the quest for food to satisfy the youngsters.

Merlins, the hunting bird of noblewomen during the Middle Ages, are shy and rare. In the early 1970s there were probably only 600–800 pairs in Britain, and because they are low-flying and do not engage in the aerobatics of other falcons they are hard to spot. However, anyone who approaches a nest soon becomes aware of the birds' presence –, the male darts to the nearest vantage point or circles round, and shrills its 'quik–ik–ik' call.

Location ___ Date ___ Time ___ Weather ___ Call ___

Behaviour ___ Field marks ___

Sketch ___

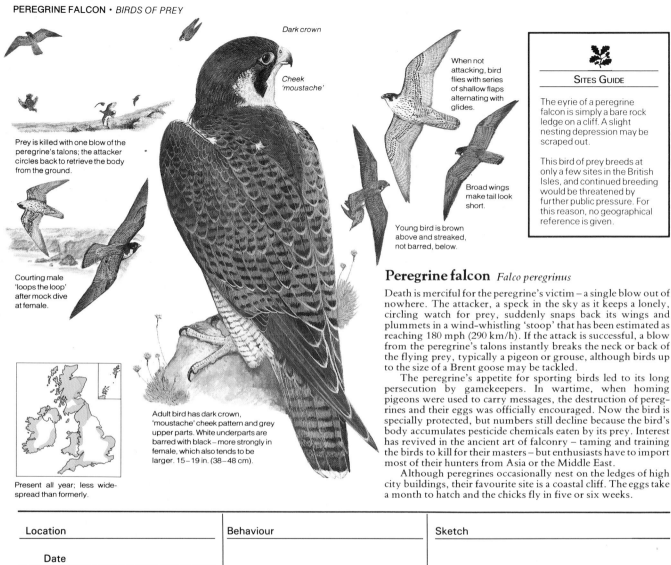

Dark crown

Cheek 'moustache'

Prey is killed with one blow of the peregrine's talons; the attacker circles back to retrieve the body from the ground.

Courting male 'loops the loop' after mock dive at female.

When not attacking, bird flies with series of shallow flaps alternating with glides.

Broad wings make tail look short.

Young bird is brown above and streaked, not barred, below.

Adult bird has dark crown, 'moustache' cheek pattern and grey upper parts. White underparts are barred with black – more strongly in female, which also tends to be larger. 15–19 in. (38–48 cm).

Present all year; less widespread than formerly.

SITES GUIDE

The eyrie of a peregrine falcon is simply a bare rock ledge on a cliff. A slight nesting depression may be scraped out.

This bird of prey breeds at only a few sites in the British Isles, and continued breeding would be threatened by further public pressure. For this reason, no geographical reference is given.

Peregrine falcon *Falco peregrinus*

Death is merciful for the peregrine's victim – a single blow out of nowhere. The attacker, a speck in the sky as it keeps a lonely, circling watch for prey, suddenly snaps back its wings and plummets in a wind-whistling 'stoop' that has been estimated as reaching 180 mph (290 km/h). If the attack is successful, a blow from the peregrine's talons instantly breaks the neck or back of the flying prey, typically a pigeon or grouse, although birds up to the size of a Brent goose may be tackled.

The peregrine's appetite for sporting birds led to its long persecution by gamekeepers. In wartime, when homing pigeons were used to carry messages, the destruction of peregrines and their eggs was officially encouraged. Now the bird is specially protected, but numbers still decline because the bird's body accumulates pesticide chemicals eaten by its prey. Interest has revived in the ancient art of falconry – taming and training the birds to kill for their masters – but enthusiasts have to import most of their hunters from Asia or the Middle East.

Although peregrines occasionally nest on the ledges of high city buildings, their favourite site is a coastal cliff. The eggs take a month to hatch and the chicks fly in five or six weeks.

Location	Behaviour	Sketch
Date		
Time		
Weather	Field marks	
Call		

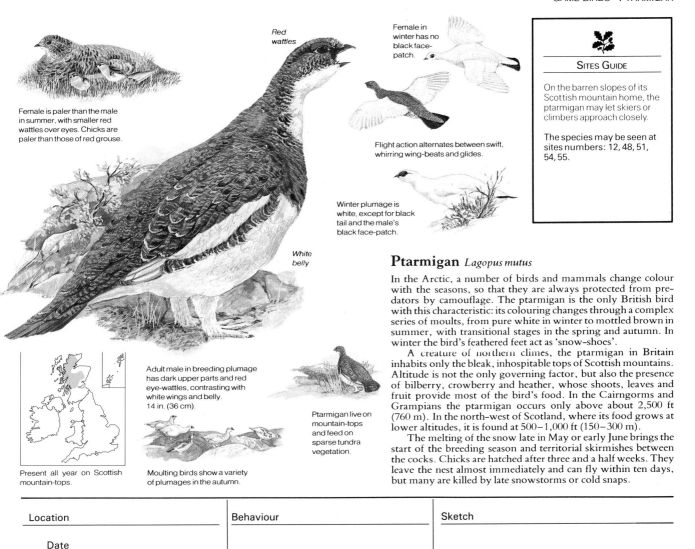

Female is paler than the male in summer, with smaller red wattles over eyes. Chicks are paler than those of red grouse.

Red wattles

Female in winter has no black face-patch.

Flight action alternates between swift, whirring wing-beats and glides.

Winter plumage is white, except for black tail and the male's black face-patch.

White belly

SITES GUIDE

On the barren slopes of its Scottish mountain home, the ptarmigan may let skiers or climbers approach closely.

The species may be seen at sites numbers: 12, 48, 51, 54, 55.

Ptarmigan *Lagopus mutus*

In the Arctic, a number of birds and mammals change colour with the seasons, so that they are always protected from predators by camouflage. The ptarmigan is the only British bird with this characteristic: its colouring changes through a complex series of moults, from pure white in winter to mottled brown in summer, with transitional stages in the spring and autumn. In winter the bird's feathered feet act as 'snow-shoes'.

A creature of northern climes, the ptarmigan in Britain inhabits only the bleak, inhospitable tops of Scottish mountains. Altitude is not the only governing factor, but also the presence of bilberry, crowberry and heather, whose shoots, leaves and fruit provide most of the bird's food. In the Cairngorms and Grampians the ptarmigan occurs only above about 2,500 ft (760 m). In the north-west of Scotland, where its food grows at lower altitudes, it is found at 500–1,000 ft (150–300 m).

The melting of the snow late in May or early June brings the start of the breeding season and territorial skirmishes between the cocks. Chicks are hatched after three and a half weeks. They leave the nest almost immediately and can fly within ten days, but many are killed by late snowstorms or cold snaps.

Present all year on Scottish mountain-tops.

Adult male in breeding plumage has dark upper parts and red eye-wattles, contrasting with white wings and belly. 14 in. (36 cm).

Ptarmigan live on mountain-tops and feed on sparse tundra vegetation.

Moulting birds show a variety of plumages in the autumn.

Location	Behaviour	Sketch
Date		
Time		
Weather	Field marks	
Call		

Red wattles

In display flight, male springs straight up, then glides down crowing loudly, flapping wings before landing.

Dark wings, body

Seen in flight, bird lacks wing-bar of black grouse.

Adult female is smaller and paler than male; chicks more deeply coloured than ptarmigan.

Present all year; stays within breeding range.

Adult male has dark reddish-brown plumage, except for red eye-wattles and white legs. 15 in. (38 cm).

Red grouse *Lagopus lagopus*

Exploding into chattering flight out of the moorland heather almost beneath one's feet, a plump and handsome red grouse is an exhilarating sight. A different sighting of the red grouse is that eagerly awaited by the hunter as beaters drive birds towards the waiting guns on August's 'Glorious Twelfth', when the grouse-shooting season opens. Stocks are maintained by managed breeding, and the systematic burning of patches of heather ensures new growth in the variety of stages that the birds need: mature vegetation for cover, young heather shoots for food and clearings where chicks can sun themselves.

The red grouse, with its 'qurrack-rack-rack' bark of an alarm call and the male's 'go-back, go-back' challenge to rivals, used to be considered an exclusively British species. Today it is classified as a 'race' – a slightly different subspecies – of the willow grouse of Europe, Asia and North America.

Six to a dozen eggs are laid in a sparsely lined ground depression, sheltered by heather or a tussock of grass. The eggs, basically creamy but thickly speckled and blotched with dark brown, hatch after three to three and a half weeks. The chicks quickly leave the nest to feed and can fly in less than two weeks.

Location	Behaviour	Sketch
Date		
Time		
Weather	Field marks	
Call		

In flight, rounded tail distinguishes both male and female from black grouse.

Bushy throat feathers

Adult male makes short display flights during the breeding season.

Adult female resembles female black grouse but is larger – 24 in. (60 cm) – with a chestnut breast. A submissive posture is adopted in courtship.

Adult male is distinguishable from other game birds by its large size, dark colouring and bushy throat feathers. Its display posture is accompanied by a characteristic qurqling song. 34 in. (86 cm).

Present all year; derived from 1830s re-introduction.

Comb-like projections beneath the toes may help the bird to walk on snow.

Displaying males are very aggressive and may threaten deer, sheep or even humans.

SITES GUIDE

The capercaillie nests on the ground, often between roots of a tree. Chicks can fly a little by about three weeks old.

The species may be seen at sites numbers: 48, 53, 55.

Capercaillie *Tetrao urogallus*

Although the capercaillie was fairly widespread in Scotland and Ireland up to the beginning of the 18th century, it had virtually been exterminated by the 1750s. This was the result of the wholesale clearance of the pine forests in which it lived, and of excessive shooting. In Scotland, the last individual birds were shot in Aberdeenshire in 1785.

It was not until 1837, when a long series of re-introductions started from Sweden, that the species was re-established throughout most of the eastern highlands of central Scotland – especially in the river valleys of the Dee, Don, Spey and Tay. Attempts at introductions into England, and re-introductions into Ireland, have not been successful.

Like the black grouse, the male capercaillie is noted for its flamboyant and aggressive courtship display and extraordinary vocal accompaniment. The call starts with a slow series of clicks which gradually speed up into a rattle; this is quickly followed by a 'klop' rather like a cork being drawn from a bottle, and by a final rustling, hissing sound. The exact derivation of the bird's peculiar name is lost in antiquity; it may come from the Gaelic word *capullcoille*, which means 'horse of the woods'.

Location	Behaviour	Sketch
Date		
Time		
Weather	Field marks	
Call		

Adult male's tail shape and white wing-bar are distinctive in flight.

Female in flight is distinguishable from red grouse by notched tail.

As immature males moult, their plumage gradually changes from brown to black.

Adult males perform communal courtship displays before the female birds. The birds are polygamous.

Lyre-shaped tail

Red wattles

Adult female is smaller than male. Her brown-barred plumage is more like that of the red grouse, but it is greyer and the tail is forked.

Adult male's black plumage, red head wattles and lyre-shaped tail make it immediately recognisable. 21 in. (53 cm).

Present all year; sedentary, rare in southern England.

Chicks are tended by the female alone. She leads them out morning and evening to feed on shoots, buds and seeds.

Sites Guide

Young grouse have a mottled reddish-buff crown and upper parts. The nest is scraped in the ground by the hen.

The species may be seen at sites numbers: 3, 11, 24, 25, 29, 35, 48, 55.

Black grouse *Lyrurus tetrix*

In the mating season, male and female black grouse gather early in the morning for a communal courtship display known as a 'lek'. The same site may be used for the display over many years. Each male holds a small area within the site, on which he stands with tail fanned and erect, wings spread and drooped. He faces a rival male and utters a prolonged, bubbling, cooing sound which is occasionally interrupted by a loud, scraping 'tcheway'.

The cock birds adopt threatening postures and frequently jump into the air. During this display, the sombre-plumaged females strut nonchalantly between the males. For most of the time, the aggression is ritualised. But sometimes full-blooded fights take place in which beaks, wings and breasts are used. After a cock bird has vanquished its rival it will turn and take on another bird. Eventually, a female may invite mating by crouching before the victorious male – which circles in front of the hen with its neck and head outstretched.

The nest of the black grouse is well hidden in grass or heather, and six to ten eggs are usually laid. The newly hatched chicks start to grow their flight feathers within three or four days, and can fly well within a month.

Location	Behaviour	Sketch
Date		
Time		
Weather	Field marks	
Call		

The bird's grating call is uttered with head pointed up and wings drooped.

The nest is a pad of dead grass built on the ground among long grass or weeds. The female alone incubates the 8–12 eggs.

Apr.–Sept. visitor; numbers gradually decreasing.

Red-brown wing patches are clearly visible in flight; the legs dangle.

During migration, flight appears stronger and legs are carried more horizontally.

Streaked upper parts

Corncrake nests and young can survive only where unmechanised methods of reaping are used.

Bill resembles a game bird's, but narrow body marks this as a rail. Upper parts are streaked, lower parts paler. Sexes are alike. 10½ in. (27 cm).

Corncrake *Crex crex*

Birdwatchers eager for a sight of this elusive bird sometimes notch a piece of wood or bone with a knife and draw a stick across it near a likely field of growing grass. The rasping sound produced is an acceptable imitation of the bird's distinctive and far-carrying rasping double call, 'aarr-aarr, aarr-aarr', repeated monotonously for long periods by day and night. A male bird that hears the imitation sometimes breaks cover in the belief that the sound comes from a rival male invading its territory.

Although fields of corn are sometimes used for breeding, the common name corncrake is less appropriate than the rarer alternative, landrail. Formerly it nested in large numbers throughout the British Isles, but it is now widespread only in Ireland and the Scottish islands and its range is still contracting in Britain and elsewhere in northern Europe. Mechanical hay-cutting has been blamed as part of the cause of the bird's decline, but it cannot be the only one.

Corncrakes' eggs are incubated mainly by the female. The blackish-brown chicks hatch after about 17 days, leave the nest in a few hours, and feed themselves after two or three days.

Location	Behaviour	Sketch
Date		
Time		
Weather	Field marks	
Call		

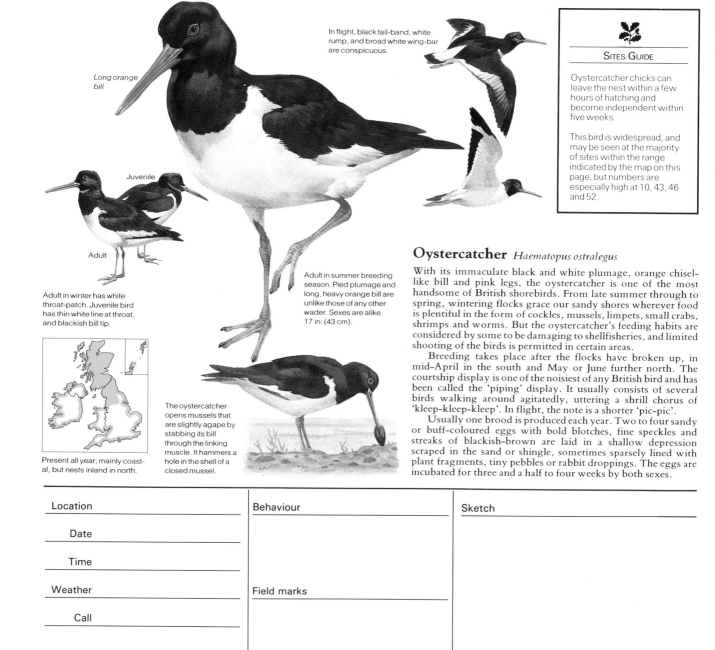

In flight, black tail-band, white rump, and broad white wing-bar are conspicuous.

Long orange bill

Juvenile

Adult

Adult in winter has white throat-patch. Juvenile bird has thin white line at throat, and blackish bill tip.

Adult in summer breeding season. Pied plumage and long, heavy orange bill are unlike those of any other wader. Sexes are alike. 17 in. (43 cm).

The oystercatcher opens mussels that are slightly agape by stabbing its bill through the linking muscle. It hammers a hole in the shell of a closed mussel.

Present all year; mainly coastal, but nests inland in north.

SITES GUIDE

Oystercatcher chicks can leave the nest within a few hours of hatching and become independent within five weeks.

This bird is widespread, and may be seen at the majority of sites within the range indicated by the map on this page, but numbers are especially high at 10, 43, 46 and 52.

Oystercatcher *Haematopus ostralegus*

With its immaculate black and white plumage, orange chisel-like bill and pink legs, the oystercatcher is one of the most handsome of British shorebirds. From late summer through to spring, wintering flocks grace our sandy shores wherever food is plentiful in the form of cockles, mussels, limpets, small crabs, shrimps and worms. But the oystercatcher's feeding habits are considered by some to be damaging to shellfisheries, and limited shooting of the birds is permitted in certain areas.

Breeding takes place after the flocks have broken up, in mid-April in the south and May or June further north. The courtship display is one of the noisiest of any British bird and has been called the 'piping' display. It usually consists of several birds walking around agitatedly, uttering a shrill chorus of 'kleep-kleep-kleep'. In flight, the note is a shorter 'pic-pic'.

Usually one brood is produced each year. Two to four sandy or buff-coloured eggs with bold blotches, fine speckles and streaks of blackish-brown are laid in a shallow depression scraped in the sand or shingle, sometimes sparsely lined with plant fragments, tiny pebbles or rabbit droppings. The eggs are incubated for three and a half to four weeks by both sexes.

Location	Behaviour	Sketch
Date		
Time		
Weather	Field marks	
Call		

White breast-band

Adult female, summer

Adult female, summer

Adult, winter

In all plumages, birds in flight show white breast-band from below.

Adult males have duller plumage than females. They assume all parental duties.

Adult female has a plump body and a small head. Its chestnut underparts and white breast-band are distinctive. 8½ in. (22 cm).

Rare May–Oct. visitor; has bred in Wales.

Juveniles lack the adult's chestnut belly, and have pale-edged feathers on their upper parts.

Adult male uses distraction display to lure predator from the eggs or young birds. It flops to the ground as though its wings are broken.

SITES GUIDE

The dotterel's nest is a scrape in the ground lined with moss and lichen. The male bird incubates the eggs.

The species may be seen at sites numbers: 11, 25, 40, 51, 55.

Dotterel *Eudromias morinellus*

This charming, tame little wader breeds on barren mountain-tops in the north and west of Britain, though in the Arctic it occurs down to sea level and in Holland it has bred on farmland below sea level. Its tameness makes it easy to catch and, before protective legislation was introduced, persecution by humans wanting to eat it or use its feathers to make fishing lures reduced its population to a low level from which it has not completely recovered. The bird's strongholds are invaded by holiday-makers, but it seems to be more than holding its own.

In the first half of May, as the snows melt above 2,500–3,000 ft (760–900 m), the nesting season gets under way with the making of a shallow scrape in the ground. After laying, the female usually loses almost all interest in her offspring, the male incubating the eggs and, after they hatch, undertaking almost all parental duties, including feeding.

Dotterels feed mainly on insects such as beetles and flies, but also eat spiders, small snails, earthworms and seeds. When the young are grown, dotterels begin their migration. Small flocks often follow the same routes every year, even turning up each spring in exactly the same group of fields.

Location	Behaviour	Sketch
Date		
Time		
Weather	Field marks	
Call		

In display flight, the male flies high with a slow, shallow wing action, uttering a distinctive melancholy song.

Gold speckles

Black belly

Foraging birds move in short runs, with pauses to pick up their food, which includes worms, slugs and seeds.

Present all year; breeders leave high moors in winter.

Adult male in summer plumage has black belly contrasting with gold-speckled upper parts. 11 in. (28 cm).

Female has less black below than male. The downy chicks have similar colouring to adults, but show more white.

Winter

Summer

From below, pale feathers are visible at the wing base at all seasons. From above, a faint wing-bar is visible, and rump appears dark.

Summer

Flocks seen in spring may include birds already in summer plumage, some of them of the northern race, blacker faced than southern race.

SITES GUIDE

The nest of the golden plover is a sparsely lined scrape on a bog hummock or grass tussock on moorland.

The species may be seen at sites numbers: 2, 11-15, 17, 24-26, 28, 30, 32, 34, 35, 40, 41, 43, 46, 51, 52, 54, 57.

Golden plover *Pluvialis apricaria*

This strikingly handsome wader produces one of the most beautiful, plaintive calls of any British bird. Its flutey 'klew-ee' call resounds over the upland moors on which it breeds in summer. The less often heard full song is a longer but equally musical double note, uttered repeatedly, 'koo-roo'. Display flight is accompanied by a sad-sounding 'perr-ee-oo, perr-ee-oo', with the emphasis on the middle syllable.

Nests are difficult to find, and so are the chicks. Only one brood is raised. The first clutches of four, or sometimes three, eggs are laid towards the end of April at two to three-day intervals. Incubation, mainly by the female, begins after the third egg and lasts for four weeks. The male remains on guard, ready to sound the alarm and set up a diversion by feigning injury. Soon after hatching, the chicks are led away from the nest and looked after by both adults for about a month, after which they become independent.

In winter, golden plovers from Iceland and Scandinavia move to southern Britain, gathering on farmland in large flocks to grub for insects and worms. In severe weather they are much less inclined to seek food on the coast than the grey plovers.

Location	Behaviour	Sketch
Date		
Time		
Weather	Field marks	
Call		

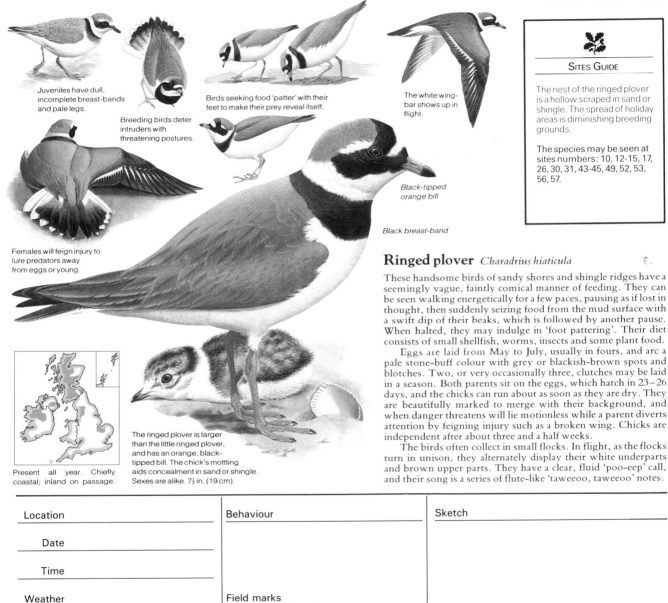

Juveniles have dull, incomplete breast-bands and pale legs.

Breeding birds deter intruders with threatening postures.

Birds seeking food 'patter' with their feet to make their prey reveal itself.

The white wing-bar shows up in flight.

Females will feign injury to lure predators away from eggs or young.

Black-tipped orange bill

Black breast-band

Present all year. Chiefly coastal; inland on passage.

The ringed plover is larger than the little ringed plover, and has an orange, black-tipped bill. The chick's mottling aids concealment in sand or shingle. Sexes are alike. 7½ in. (19 cm).

Ringed plover *Charadrius hiaticula*

These handsome birds of sandy shores and shingle ridges have a seemingly vague, faintly comical manner of feeding. They can be seen walking energetically for a few paces, pausing as if lost in thought, then suddenly seizing food from the mud surface with a swift dip of their beaks, which is followed by another pause. When halted, they may indulge in 'foot pattering'. Their diet consists of small shellfish, worms, insects and some plant food.

Eggs are laid from May to July, usually in fours, and are a pale stone-buff colour with grey or blackish-brown spots and blotches. Two, or very occasionally three, clutches may be laid in a season. Both parents sit on the eggs, which hatch in 23–26 days, and the chicks can run about as soon as they are dry. They are beautifully marked to merge with their background, and when danger threatens will lie motionless while a parent diverts attention by feigning injury such as a broken wing. Chicks are independent after about three and a half weeks.

The birds often collect in small flocks. In flight, as the flocks turn in unison, they alternately display their white underparts and brown upper parts. They have a clear, fluid 'poo-eep' call, and their song is a series of flute-like 'taweeoo, taweeoo' notes.

Location	Behaviour	Sketch
Date		
Time		
Weather	Field marks	
Call		

In winter, upper parts are a dull black-brown and there is much less white on the head.

Mainly winter visitor; some non-breeders in summer.

Orange legs

In summer, upper parts of adult bird appear tortoise-shell, while head is mainly white. Legs are orange, and bill is black. Sexes are alike. 9 in. (23 cm).

Stones are turned over, and fine seaweed is rolled up with bill to locate food.

White head

In flight, the complex 'harlequin' pattern of black, white and brown in the turnstone's plumage shows clearly. It is unlike that of any other wader.

SITES GUIDE

Rocks exposed at low tide are a common feeding ground for groups of turnstones, most numerous in autumn and spring.

The species may be seen at sites numbers: 2, 5, 10, 12, 14, 15, 18, 19, 26, 30, 31, 43, 44, 47.

Turnstone *Arenaria interpres*

This colourful black, white and chestnut wader quickly reveals the origin of its name as it walks across the sands and rocks at low tide in search of food. Not only stones but also seaweed, shells and driftwood are diligently lifted by its probing bill in the hope of finding sandhoppers and other small shore-life.

In Britain, the turnstone is a passage migrant in autumn and spring, on its way to and from its summer breeding grounds in the Arctic. It often winters in coastal areas, and some birds stay for the summer on the north-east coast of Scotland, though not to breed. Turnstones usually breed on islands, choosing rocky and stony ground for their nests which are no more than shallow scrapes in the ground lined with lichen, grasses and leaves. Three to five greenish eggs with blackish-brown spots are laid, and both parents share in the incubation. The eggs hatch after 22–23 days, and the chicks are able to feed themselves within a day. Young birds resemble winter adults, but are duller.

When feeding, the turnstone's back is an excellent camouflage against the background of stones and seaweed, but when disturbed it flies up showing its black-and-white wing pattern and emitting a twittering 'titititit'.

Location	Behaviour	Sketch
Date		
Time		
Weather	Field marks	
Call		

In winter plumage, flying birds show a faint white wing-bar above, and prominent black spot at base of each wing below. In summer plumage, black underparts are visible.

Winter

Summer

Winter

Grey plumage

Adult in winter is mottled grey and white. Bill is heavier than golden plover's. Sexes alike. 11 in. (28 cm).

Winter visitor to estuaries; a few remain in summer.

Adult in summer; chequered black-and-white plumage appears from late spring.

Birds forage like golden plovers, often catching small crabs.

At high tide plovers at different stages of moult roost in flocks on sand bars or a short distance inland.

The grey plover's hunched posture contrasts with the golden plover's sprightly, upright stance.

Sites Guide

Grey plovers are often seen feeding in shallow water, particularly by the seashore and mud-flats.

The species may be seen at sites numbers: 10-15, 17, 18, 26, 30, 32, 45, 49, 57.

Grey plover *Pluvialis squatarola*

Two medium-sized birds with pale greyish upper parts, white underparts and dark grey legs are feeding near a coastal pool in winter. When disturbed they take off, call with a musical 'pee-oo-ee' and fly with strong, direct flight out over the salt-marsh. The conspicuous black axillaries, or 'arm-pits', remove any doubt that the birds are grey plovers.

Grey plovers breed in the high Arctic tundras of Canada and Russia, and it is only for the autumn and winter that most birds visit Britain, although a few non-breeding birds stay over summer. Usually they are seen in twos and threes or in small groups foraging along the seashore or on estuary mud-flats.

For most of their stay in Britain these birds are dressed in their drab grey winter plumage, but in their Arctic breeding grounds they assume a striking summer plumage in which the entire face, breast and belly are black. As with most waders, grey plovers lay eggs that contain a large reserve of food, permitting the young to hatch out well enough developed to leave the nest quickly. Such species are called nidifugous, unlike nidicolous species which are hatched helpless and remain in the nest for some time.

Location	Behaviour	Sketch
Date		
Time		
Weather	Field marks	
Call		

Adult,
summer

In flight, the bird shows
a narrow white wing-
bar, and its rump
appears nearly white.

Adult,
winter

Grey above

Adult in winter plumage:
a portly bird, with grey
upper parts, white underparts
and pale legs. Sexes are alike
10 in. (25 cm).

White
below

Pale
legs

Winter visitor to sandy estuaries; coastal in summer.

Juveniles have pale-edged
feathers on their upper parts.
Knots characteristically feed
in densely packed flocks.

Flocks in flight perform spectacular
co-ordinated evolutions, appearing
darker as upper parts show, then
silvery as they turn.

Adult bird in early autumn
has remains of brick-red
breeding plumage.

SITES GUIDE

Knots gather at their high-tide
roosting places on mud-
banks, often with the larger,
longer-billed godwits.

The species may be seen at
sites numbers: 12-15, 17, 18,
31, 43, 45, 46, 49, 53, 57.

Knot *Calidris canutus*

King Canute, the Viking who ruled England in the 11th century, is said to have been very fond of the wader known today as
the knot. The bird was later likened to a tiny Canute standing on
the shore and ordering the tide to go back as the monarch was
supposed to have done. According to a 17th-century work on
ornithology, Canute called the bird the 'knout'.

The 17th-century writer Sir Thomas Browne referred to the
bird as the 'knot', or 'gnatt', which could stem from the
similarity between a distant flock of knots and a swarm of gnats.
Less fancifully, the bird was probably named after its cry, a
low-pitched 'knut' – which, when uttered by a dense flock,
becomes a continuous low twitter. Another, mellower note is a
higher-pitched whistle-like 'twit-twit'.

Enormous numbers of knots pass through Britain in the
autumn and spring, and many of them winter on the west coast
of Africa. Some knots stay behind and provide one of the
winter's great bird spectacles – especially when they perform
their elaborate, group aerobatics. While on shore, they feed on
crustaceans, molluscs, worms and insects and roam rapidly over
the sand or mud, looking like dark, moving patches.

Location	Behaviour	Sketch
Date		
Time		
Weather	Field marks	
Call		

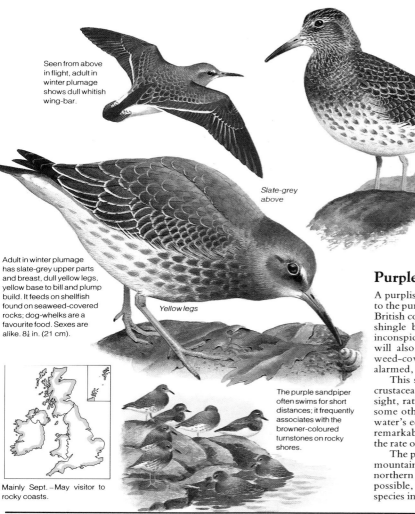

Seen from above in flight, adult in winter plumage shows dull whitish wing-bar.

Slate-grey above

Adult in winter plumage has slate-grey upper parts and breast, dull yellow legs, yellow base to bill and plump build. It feeds on shellfish found on seaweed-covered rocks; dog-whelks are a favourite food. Sexes are alike. 8¼ in. (21 cm).

Yellow legs

The purple sandpiper often swims for short distances; it frequently associates with the browner-coloured turnstones on rocky shores.

Summer plumage is more variegated than winter, with some red-brown above.

Mainly Sept. – May visitor to rocky coasts.

Sites Guide

The purple sandpiper is most commonly seen in northern Britain, searching for shellfish on offshore rocks.

The species may be seen at sites numbers: 9, 10, 19, 44, 47, 65.

Purple sandpiper *Calidris maritima*

A purplish gloss on the plumage of its upper parts gives its name to the purple sandpiper, a passage migrant and a winter visitor to British coasts. It prefers rocky shores, but is also seen on sand or shingle beaches. The pattern of its plumage makes it blend inconspicuously with beach boulders, but it is a tame bird that will also frequent the haunts of man such as harbours and weed-covered groynes and slipways, especially at high tide. If alarmed, it will fly off silently, or with a low, piping cry.

This stockier relative of the dunlin feeds mainly on insects, crustaceans, spiders, molluscs and worms. It finds its prey by sight, rather than probing with its beak to find it by touch like some other waders. The bird's technique is to forage near the water's edge, advancing and retreating with the tide. It can be a remarkably fast feeder, sometimes picking up items of food at the rate of one every one or two seconds.

The purple sandpiper's principal breeding grounds – tundra, mountains and upland fells – are fairly close to Britain, in northern Scandinavia, the Faeroe Islands and Iceland. It is possible, therefore, that it may become a regular breeding species in the British Isles.

Location	Behaviour	Sketch
Date		
Time		
Weather	Field marks	
Call		

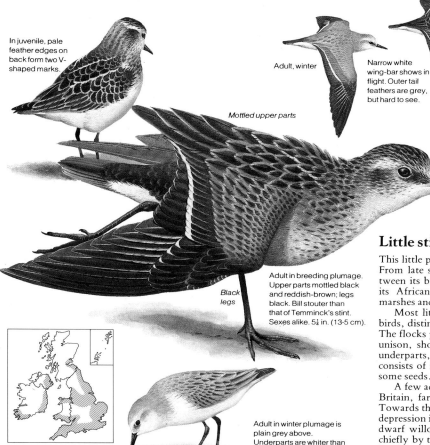

In juvenile, pale feather edges on back form two V-shaped marks.

Adult, winter

Mottled upper parts

Narrow white wing-bar shows in flight. Outer tail feathers are grey, but hard to see.

Adult, summer

Adult in breeding plumage. Upper parts mottled black and reddish-brown; legs black. Bill stouter than that of Temminck's stint. Sexes alike. 5¼ in. (13·5 cm).

Black legs

Aug.–Sept. passage migrant; may winter in Britain.

Adult in winter plumage is plain grey above. Underparts are whiter than in Temminck's stint. The breast is faintly streaked.

Sites Guide

Little stints obtain their food on or near the surface of the mud, picking or probing for small shellfish and worms.

The species may be seen at sites numbers: 2, 12, 14, 15, 17, 18, 44, 45, 49, 53.

Little stint *Calidris minuta*

This little passage migrant is the smallest wader seen in Britain. From late summer to early November it passes through, between its breeding grounds in northern Russia and Siberia and its African wintering grounds, and inhabits inland lakes, marshes and sewage farms, and coastal sand and mud-flats.

Most little stints recorded in Britain in autumn are young birds, distinguished by two pronounced V-shapes on the back. The flocks perform aerial manoeuvres, twisting and turning in unison, showing first their upper parts and then their white underparts, the whole flock seeming to change colour. The diet consists of insects and their larvae, small shellfish, worms and some seeds. The call is a short 'chit, chit'.

A few adult birds in breeding plumage are sometimes seen in Britain, far from their breeding habitat in tundra or marsh. Towards the beginning of July a nest-scrape is made in a shallow depression in the ground and lined with dead leaves of plants like dwarf willow. Four eggs are usually laid; these are incubated chiefly by the male, which also takes the major share of caring for the young. The broods soon form into flocks, the young and old birds usually migrating separately.

Location	Behaviour	Sketch
Date		
Time		
Weather	Field marks	
Call		

Adult, summer

Adult, winter

In flight, the sanderling is low, swift and direct. Both in winter and in summer plumage it displays a conspicuous white wing-bar.

Dark shoulder

Black legs

Adult sanderling in winter plumage is pale grey above, with dark shoulder mark. Legs are black. Sexes are alike. 8 in. (20 cm).

Plumage of young birds resembles winter garb of adults, but has a pinkish tinge.

Winter visitor to sandy coasts, sometimes inland.

Adult bird in summer breeding season develops a chequered, reddish-black pattern on upper parts and breast.

Sites Guide

Sanderlings usually feed in parties, sometimes mingling with other waders. They prefer sandy shores to mud.

The species may be seen at sites numbers: 10, 12-15, 17, 43, 45, 59.

Sanderling *Calidris alba*

With frenetic bursts of energy, flocks of sanderlings scurry along the seashore, their heads down in pursuit of retreating waves. They snatch a few morsels of food then race back in advance of the next wave to avoid getting washed off their feet. If disturbed they rise with a chorus of liquid 'twick, twick, twick' calls and move further along the beach to resume their feeding.

In winter, sanderlings can be seen on most sandy shores in Britain, but in the summer they are birds of the high Arctic where they breed. The nest is a neat and fairly deep cut, scraped in the ground near a clump of willow or other vegetation and lined with a deep layer of leaves. The usual clutch of eggs is four; coloured pale olive-green or sometimes brownish, with a sprinkling of fine, brown speckles and occasionally a few tiny black spots or streaks.

When danger threatens, one of the parents feigns injury, a common device among waders. The bird scuttles along the ground fluttering its wings as if they are broken, so distracting the predator from the nest. It flies up only if the predator approaches too close.

Location	Behaviour	Sketch
Date		
Time		
Weather	Field marks	
Call		

Feeding birds leave a trail of probe marks, made with a rapid sewing-machine-like action of the beak while on the move.

At high tide, huge flocks fly along the shore, moving in unison and looking from a distance like clouds of smoke.

Winter plumage is brown-grey above, white below with darker breast. Juveniles are similar. Bill length varies but is usually shorter than in curlew sandpiper.

Red-brown and black back

Adult, winter

Adult, summer

In flight, at all seasons, wing shows white wing-bar; tail and rump dark with white edges.

In breeding plumage, adult's distinguishing features are black belly and red-brown and black back. Young are white below and brown and black above. Sexes are alike. 7 in. (18 cm).

Black belly

Present all year; mainly round coasts in winter.

Dunlin *Calidris alpina*

When crossing damp moors in the Pennines or upland Scotland, it is easy to overlook the unobtrusive dunlins that breed there in considerable numbers. Dunlins are never dense on the ground and tend to keep their distance, watching silently from afar.

A purring trill is often the first clue to the bird's presence. During its song the dunlin circles over its territory at heights of up to 200 ft (60 m), either gliding with wings partly raised, or else hovering, rising and falling as it does so. Sometimes several birds take part in aerial chases, darting rapidly about, and twisting and turning abruptly.

The dunlin's nest is a neat little cup, in a hollow in a grass tussock. Normally four eggs are laid, which vary in colour from pale greenish-blue to brown. The markings also vary, from tiny stipplings to heavy blotchings of chestnut or chocolate-brown. The eggs are incubated by both birds, and hatch after three weeks. In winter, dunlins often feed on coastal mud-flats, where they live on flies, molluscs, crustaceans and worms. With its head constantly bowed, the dunlin probes the mud with its bill for food. When it finds its prey it seizes and swallows it immediately, with little break in its insistent probing.

Location	Behaviour	Sketch
Date		
Time		
Weather	Field marks	
Call		

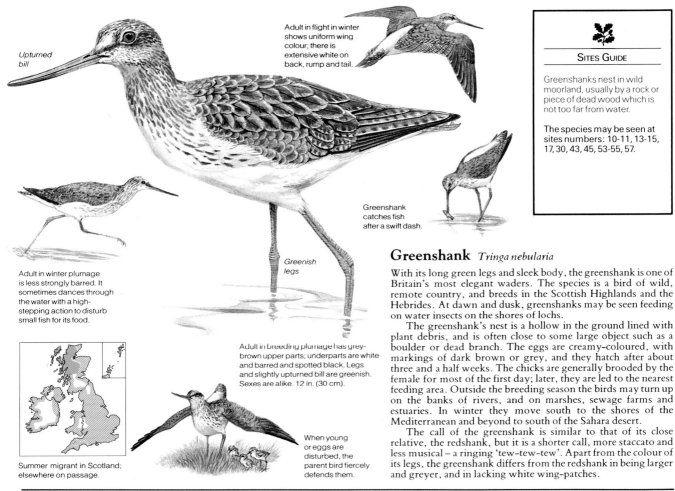

Upturned bill

Adult in flight in winter shows uniform wing colour; there is extensive white on back, rump and tail.

SITES GUIDE

Greenshanks nest in wild moorland, usually by a rock or piece of dead wood which is not too far from water.

The species may be seen at sites numbers: 10-11, 13-15, 17, 30, 43, 45, 53-55, 57.

Greenshank catches fish after a swift dash.

Adult in winter plumage is less strongly barred. It sometimes dances through the water with a high-stepping action to disturb small fish for its food.

Greenish legs

Adult in breeding plumage has grey-brown upper parts; underparts are white and barred and spotted black. Legs and slightly upturned bill are greenish. Sexes are alike. 12 in. (30 cm).

Summer migrant in Scotland; elsewhere on passage.

When young or eggs are disturbed, the parent bird fiercely defends them.

Greenshank *Tringa nebularia*

With its long green legs and sleek body, the greenshank is one of Britain's most elegant waders. The species is a bird of wild, remote country, and breeds in the Scottish Highlands and the Hebrides. At dawn and dusk, greenshanks may be seen feeding on water insects on the shores of lochs.

The greenshank's nest is a hollow in the ground lined with plant debris, and is often close to some large object such as a boulder or dead branch. The eggs are creamy-coloured, with markings of dark brown or grey, and they hatch after about three and a half weeks. The chicks are generally brooded by the female for most of the first day; later, they are led to the nearest feeding area. Outside the breeding season the birds may turn up on the banks of rivers, and on marshes, sewage farms and estuaries. In winter they move south to the shores of the Mediterranean and beyond to south of the Sahara desert.

The call of the greenshank is similar to that of its close relative, the redshank, but it is a shorter call, more staccato and less musical – a ringing 'tew-tew-tew'. Apart from the colour of its legs, the greenshank differs from the redshank in being larger and greyer, and in lacking white wing-patches.

Location	Behaviour	Sketch
Date		
Time		
Weather	Field marks	
Call		

White wing-patches

Adult in breeding plumage has orange-red legs; in flight, large white wing-patch is conspicuous. Tail is barred black and white. Sexes are alike. 11 in. (28 cm).

Orange-red legs

Present all year; winters chiefly on coasts.

Adult winter plumage is less strongly streaked. Most food is obtained from estuary mud. When feeding, the bill tip just touches the surface.

Redshanks perform a characteristic 'alarm' flight when intruders threaten a nest or young in the area.

Young birds remain in dense marsh vegetation until old enough to fly. They are guarded by the mother.

SITES GUIDE

Redshanks and dunlins frequently gather together on the tideline in winter to feed on small marine life such as shellfish.

The species may be seen at sites numbers: 2, 10, 12-14, 17, 18, 20, 26, 30-32, 34, 40, 41, 43, 46, 47, 49, 53, 57, 59.

Redshank *Tringa totanus*

Extreme alertness has earned the redshank the description of 'sentinel of the marsh'. A hysterical volley of harsh, piping notes sounds the alarm as soon as any intruder approaches. This piercing warning contrasts sharply with the bird's musical and liquid 'tew-ew-ew' call at other times.

During its display flight the redshank utters a fluting 'tee-woo-tee-woo-tee-woo' song or a long succession of 'teu, teu, teu' notes as it rises and falls on quivering wings. On alighting, the bird often leaves its wings stretched vertically over its back, displaying the white undersides. The redshank begins to breed from the middle of April onwards, nesting amongst the grass in a shallow, lined hollow in the ground. There it lays three or four darkly speckled, creamy eggs. Both adults incubate the eggs, which hatch after about three and a half weeks.

Redshanks inhabit a variety of grassy meadows, river meadows and marshes. When winter comes many move to the coast, especially to the salt-marshes where they often congregate in flocks many hundreds strong. The birds live off all sorts of invertebrates, some small fish and frogs, and a certain amount of seeds, buds and berries.

Location	Behaviour	Sketch
Date		
Time		
Weather	Field marks	
Call		

Flocks sometimes plunge down in erratic spirals, or 'whiffle', like pink-footed geese.

Russet underparts

Barred tail

Adult in winter.

Adult in summer.

In flight, bar-tailed godwit shows extensive white rump and barred tail, but no wing-bar. Slightly upturned bill is distinctive.

Bird often makes swift probe for food, walking on round its bill almost without pausing.

Passage migrant and winter visitor; a few in summer.

Adult in winter plumage. Upper parts are more streaked than in black-tailed godwit, and legs are shorter. This bird wades less, walks more briskly.

Adult in summer plumage. Russet underparts extending to under-tail coverts distinguish this bird from black-tailed godwit in breeding season. Tail is barred. Sexes are alike. 15 in. (38 cm).

Sites Guide

In winter, bar-tailed godwits are often seen in large flocks on the tideline, in company with other waders.

The species may be seen at sites numbers: 10, 12-15, 17, 18, 31, 43, 45, 49, 53, 57, 59.

Bar-tailed godwit *Limosa lapponica*

Anglo-Saxons appear to have regarded the godwit as a table delicacy, for the name they gave the bird, *god wiht*, meant 'good creature' and implies a respect for its eating qualities. Nowadays, however, the godwits have nothing to fear from man.

Unlike its close relative the black-tailed godwit, the bar-tailed godwit does not breed in Britain. Its nearest breeding grounds are in Scandinavia, beyond the tree line on the open swampy tundra, with scattered pools. Flocks of 'bar-tails' pass through Britain's mud-flats and estuaries in autumn and spring, but rarely venture inland. Some non-breeding birds stay for the summer, and many stay all the winter, when flocks may be seen probing for small crabs, shrimps, sandhoppers and marine worms. In summer, insects form a large part of the bird's diet.

Outside the breeding season, bar-tailed godwits are usually seen in flocks, when their medium size, long legs and very long, slightly upturned bills make them unmistakable for any other bird except the black-tailed godwit; however, 'black-tails' have a prominent white wing-bar, conspicuous in flight, which the bar-tail lacks. Flocks of bar-tails may sometimes be quite noisy, producing a chorus of reedy 'kirruc' calls.

Location	Behaviour	Sketch
Date		
Time		
Weather	Field marks	
Call		

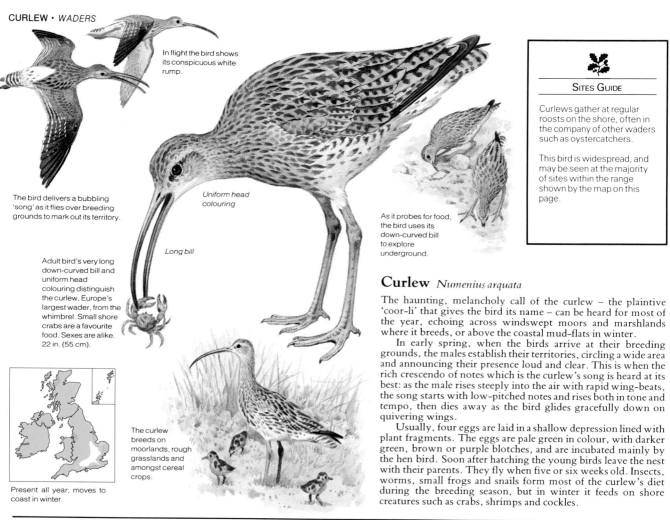

In flight the bird shows its conspicuous white rump.

The bird delivers a bubbling 'song' as it flies over breeding grounds to mark out its territory.

Uniform head colouring

Long bill

Adult bird's very long down-curved bill and uniform head colouring distinguish the curlew, Europe's largest wader, from the whimbrel. Small shore crabs are a favourite food. Sexes are alike. 22 in. (55 cm).

As it probes for food, the bird uses its down-curved bill to explore underground.

The curlew breeds on moorlands, rough grasslands and amongst cereal crops.

Present all year; moves to coast in winter.

SITES GUIDE

Curlews gather at regular roosts on the shore, often in the company of other waders such as oystercatchers.

This bird is widespread, and may be seen at the majority of sites within the range shown by the map on this page.

Curlew *Numenius arquata*

The haunting, melancholy call of the curlew – the plaintive 'coor-li' that gives the bird its name – can be heard for most of the year, echoing across windswept moors and marshlands where it breeds, or above the coastal mud-flats in winter.

In early spring, when the birds arrive at their breeding grounds, the males establish their territories, circling a wide area and announcing their presence loud and clear. This is when the rich crescendo of notes which is the curlew's song is heard at its best: as the male rises steeply into the air with rapid wing-beats, the song starts with low-pitched notes and rises both in tone and tempo, then dies away as the bird glides gracefully down on quivering wings.

Usually, four eggs are laid in a shallow depression lined with plant fragments. The eggs are pale green in colour, with darker green, brown or purple blotches, and are incubated mainly by the hen bird. Soon after hatching the young birds leave the nest with their parents. They fly when five or six weeks old. Insects, worms, small frogs and snails form most of the curlew's diet during the breeding season, but in winter it feeds on shore creatures such as crabs, shrimps and cockles.

Location	Behaviour	Sketch
Date		
Time		
Weather	Field marks	
Call		

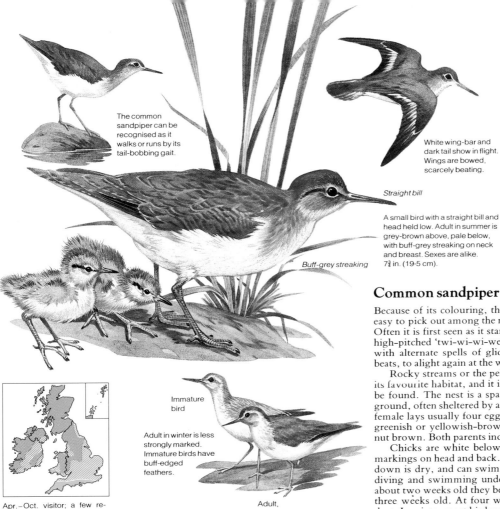

The common sandpiper can be recognised as it walks or runs by its tail-bobbing gait.

White wing-bar and dark tail show in flight. Wings are bowed, scarcely beating.

Straight bill

A small bird with a straight bill and head held low. Adult in summer is grey-brown above, pale below, with buff-grey streaking on neck and breast. Sexes are alike. 7¾ in. (19·5 cm).

Buff-grey streaking

Immature bird

Adult in winter is less strongly marked. Immature birds have buff-edged feathers.

Adult, winter

Apr.–Oct. visitor; a few remain in winter.

SITES GUIDE

The long bill of the common sandpiper is used for probing in the mud beside water for small shellfish and worms. Insects and frogs are also eaten.

The species may be seen at sites numbers: 10-12, 24, 25, 29, 32, 34-36, 39, 41, 48, 51.

Common sandpiper *Actitis hypoleucos*

Because of its colouring, the common sandpiper is not always easy to pick out among the rocks and stones of a lake shoreline. Often it is first seen as it starts into flight with a loud, musical, high-pitched 'twi-wi-wi-wee', flying low just above the water with alternate spells of gliding and flickering shallow wing-beats, to alight again at the water's edge some distance away.

Rocky streams or the pebbly shore of a lake or reservoir are its favourite habitat, and it is often common where these are to be found. The nest is a sparsely lined hollow or scrape in the ground, often sheltered by a plant or bush. About mid-May the female lays usually four eggs, which vary from creamy-buff to greenish or yellowish-brown, stippled or speckled with chestnut brown. Both parents incubate them for 20–23 days.

Chicks are white below and buff above, with a few dark markings on head and back. They leave the nest as soon as their down is dry, and can swim and feed almost at once, including diving and swimming under water to escape enemies. When about two weeks old they begin flying, and are fully airborne at three weeks old. At four weeks they are completely independent. In winter most birds migrate south to Africa.

Location	Behaviour	Sketch
Date		
Time		
Weather	Field marks	
Call		

59

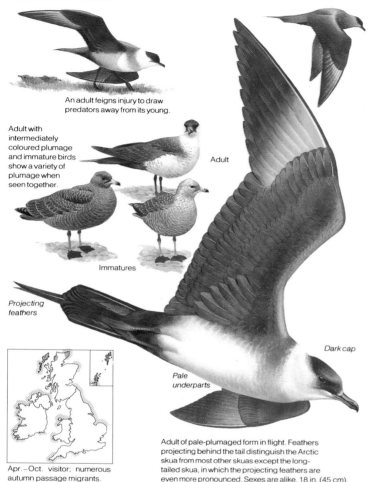

An adult feigns injury to draw predators away from its young.

Adult with intermediately coloured plumage and immature birds show a variety of plumage when seen together.

Adult

Immatures

Projecting feathers

Dark cap

Pale underparts

Dark-plumaged adults are a deeper brown, with dark underparts. They are smaller than the otherwise similar great skua, with less-prominent wing-patches.

The Arctic tern is a favourite victim of the skua, often pursued by two or more and forced to disgorge food.

Sites Guide

Arctic skuas breed in colonies on moorland, where they can be seen indulging in spectacular flights and chases.

The species may be seen at sites numbers: 12, 18, 19, 44, 47, 49, 53.

Apr.–Oct. visitor; numerous autumn passage migrants.

Adult of pale-plumaged form in flight. Feathers projecting behind the tail distinguish the Arctic skua from most other skuas except the long-tailed skua, in which the projecting feathers are even more pronounced. Sexes are alike. 18 in. (45 cm).

Arctic skua *Stercorarius parasiticus*

No bird's nest is safe from the Arctic skua, which feasts on both eggs and young. It usually hunts alone, and is savage and determined enough to scare away birds much bigger than itself. But sometimes the male and female form a team, when one bird will fight off a pair of puffins or kittiwakes, for example, while its mate plunders the nest. Like other skuas, it will steal another seabird's most recent meal by forcing it to disgorge.

Unlike the long-tailed and pomarine skuas, the Arctic skua breeds in Britain. Its nesting grounds are mainly windswept moors in Orkney and Shetland, with smaller colonies in the Hebrides and on the northern tip of mainland Scotland. The nest is often placed near a rock, hillock or tussock which is used as a look-out. Like the nests of other skuas, it is often no more than a shallow depression in the ground – or vegetation on the ground – and is scantily lined with grass, heather, moss or lichen.

A single clutch, usually of two eggs, is laid in late May or early June. The eggs are greenish-brown or buff, and are spotted and blotched with various shades of brown and grey. Incubation takes 24–28 days. The chicks are tended by both parents. They fly after one month and are independent in about two months.

Location	Behaviour	Sketch
Date		
Time		
Weather	Field marks	
Call		

Adult

On adult bird, the white wing-patch is prominent in flight, which is usually more ponderous than that of other skuas.

Immature

Kittiwake chicks often fall victim to the great skua's powerful bill.

Skua harries other seabirds to steal food.

Gannets are forced into the sea to disgorge their food.

This fierce bird viciously attacks intruders in its nesting area, striking with its feet in a head-on swoop.

White wing-patch

Brown underparts

Mainly Apr.–Sept. visitor; occasionally in winter.

Adult in characteristic aggressive display posture, wings held up and back, beak wide open. Plumage is brown, with white wing-patches and pale streaking on upper parts. Sexes are alike. 23 in. (58 cm).

Sites Guide

The great skua breeds in colonies on bare ground or moorland. The nest is a simple depression, lined with lichens.

The species may be seen at sites numbers: 1, 9, 12, 44 and 49.

Great skua *Stercorarius skua*

All skuas are pirates, and none is better equipped for the part than the great skua. This brute of a bird is not only sturdily built, aggressive and bullying, but is also the biggest of the skuas, well able to rob really large birds of their latest meals.

The great skua's favourite victim is the gannet, the large white seabird that nests on islands off the coasts of the British Isles. The skua seizes the gannet by the wingtip, so making it stall and fall into the sea. The gannet then disgorges its food and the spoils are snapped up by the waiting skua.

In the Shetland Isles, where the great skua has its main breeding grounds, the bird is known as the bonxie. The word is used by Shetlanders to describe a stout and bullying sort of person, and is so appropriate to the great skua that birdwatchers apply the term to the bird more and more widely. All intruders at a great skua's nest are 'dive-bombed' – buffeted with the bonxie's webbed feet and pecked viciously in repeated swoops. Bonxies will even land on the heads of trespassing sheep, battering them with their wings and driving them from the colony. At first the chicks are brooded by the female while the male brings food; later they are fed by both parents.

Location	Behaviour	Sketch
Date		
Time		
Weather	Field marks	
Call		

Brown head

Dark red bill

Adult in winter: all that remains of the dark hood of its breeding plumage is a dark spot behind the eye.

Immature bird

Adult, winter

Wings have white fore-edge, black tips, all year. Immature birds have darkish band across wing.

Adult in breeding plumage. The 'black' head (in fact chocolate brown) is distinctive, as are the dark red bill and legs. Sexes are alike. 14–15 in. (36–38 cm).

Young birds have more grey in plumage than larger gull species at the same age.

Flocks of birds follow ploughs and harrows to capture insects exposed in the turned-up soil.

Present all year; many birds from Europe winter here.

Sites Guide

In southern Britain, inland sites such as reservoirs are often homes for colonies of black-headed gulls.

The species may be seen at sites numbers: 1, 5, 9-14, 19, 24-27, 32, 34-36, 41, 64.

Black-headed gull *Larus ridibundus*

Of all the British gulls, the black-headed gull least deserves the description of 'sea-gull'. A recent survey showed that out of a total British population of some 300,000 pairs, only about a quarter nested on the coast. Meanwhile numerous colonies, some numbering many thousands of birds, were found inland, particularly in the north, usually in boggy areas around lakes.

In the south a higher proportion of colonies are on the coast, especially on salt marshes or among sand dunes. But even in the south the black-headed gull sometimes nests inland, on gravel or clay pits or on sewage farms.

The voice of the black-headed gull consists of a series of extremely harsh and rasping notes, and the sound of a colony in full cry is overpowering. The nest is a slight platform of vegetation or a sparsely lined scrape in the ground. There are normally three eggs, laid daily from mid-April onwards. Both parents incubate the eggs, for a total period of slightly more than three weeks. If danger threatens, the adults give the alarm and the young hide in the nearest cover or flatten motionless on the ground. The black-headed gull will eat almost anything, from fish and worms to grass, seaweed and refuse.

Location	Behaviour	Sketch
Date		
Time		
Weather	Field marks	
Call		

Yellow-green bill

In flight, kittiwakes are buoyant and graceful. Adults have solid black wingtips; juveniles show diagonal black wing-bars.

Kittiwakes usually form large colonies on inaccessible cliff ledges.

The slenderly built kittiwake has dark eyes, a yellow-green bill and black legs. The inside of the mouth is bright red. Sexes are alike. 16 in. (40 cm).

Present offshore throughout year; rarely far inland.

Fish or fish remains are taken from the surface when the kittiwake is in flight or while swimming.

Black bars on the wings and a black half-collar distinguish juvenile birds.

SITES GUIDE

Kittiwakes are not noisy birds away from their breeding grounds, but a pair at their nest will defy all comers with their cries.

The species may be seen at sites numbers: 1, 3, 4, 5, 12, 13, 18-20, 23, 44, 47, 50, 52, 61, 63.

Kittiwake *Rissa tridactyla*

No one visiting a colony of these gulls will be left in any doubt about the origin of their name, as the strident cry of 'kitti-wa-a-k' rises on all sides. Some half a million or so pairs of kittiwakes breed in Britain and Ireland, mainly along coasts in the north and west. There has been an enormous growth in the gull's population during this century, since it was given legal protection. Before that, the kittiwake was slaughtered for sport and to supply feathers for Victorian ladies' hats.

The birds usually make their homes on projecting ledges of rock on cliff faces. The nests are neat, cup-shaped structures of moss, seaweed and other plant material, cemented together with considerable quantities of droppings. The birds consolidate this with the constant paddling of their webbed feet. A typical clutch consists of two, or occasionally three, pale bluish-grey, brownish, or stone-coloured eggs with ash-grey and rich brown spots and blotches. The chicks are mainly creamy white, with greyish-brown upper parts. Both parents feed the chicks during the five to eight weeks that they spend in the nest.

The kittiwake spends its time outside the breeding season at sea, and lives on small fish, small squids, molluscs and shrimps.

Location	Behaviour	Sketch
Date		
Time		
Weather	Field marks	
Call		

Adult bird in winter plumage has grey-brown streaking on head. Underparts are white, bill and legs yellow-green and wingtips black with white spots. Sexes are alike. 16 in. (40 cm).

Black and white wingtips

Yellow-green bill

Yellow-green legs

Common gulls, like skuas, sometimes pursue other seabirds to rob them of food.

Present all year; many winter birds come from Europe.

Dark eye and yellow-green bill distinguish common gull from larger herring gull.

Adult

Adult

First-year birds

In flight, long and pointed wings typical of all gulls are conspicuous. Young birds have clear white tail with black band near tip.

First-year bird

At rest, wingtips project well beyond tail. Young bird has black-tipped bill.

SITES GUIDE

The nest of the common gull, always built on the ground, is usually sited on a marsh or moor near the sea, or on an islet or shingle beach.

The species may be seen at sites numbers: 1, 2, 9, 10, 13, 16, 25-27, 34, 41, 57, 58, 64.

Common gull *Larus canus*

In spite of its name the common gull is not common, except in north-west Ireland and Scotland. The common gull's shrill, high-pitched 'keeeeyar' echoes above inland waters as well as sea-coasts. Its colonies – which are seldom large or dense – may be on large rocks or islets in lochs, on boggy areas of grass or moorland, on beaches or on offshore islands.

The nest, which varies a great deal in size, consists of a small hollow lined with whatever plant material is available. There are usually three eggs in a clutch; they are olive-green, with blotches and streaks of dark orange-brown. Although the female does most of the nest-building, both sexes share the task of incubating the eggs, which takes three to three and a half weeks. The chicks, which are buff above and yellowish beneath, fly after about four to five weeks, but stay near the nest.

The bird's diet is very varied. Inland, it eats insects and earthworms, sometimes picked up from behind the plough, and also seeds; on the coast, crustaceans, marine worms, starfish, molluscs and shore refuse are eaten. Like many of its close relatives, the common gull also takes small mammals, the young and eggs of other birds, and even small adult birds.

Location	Behaviour	Sketch
Date		
Time		
Weather	Field marks	
Call		

Heavy bill

Young birds have whiter heads and underparts than young lesser black-backed gulls and herring gulls.

Heavy build and stout bill are conspicuous in flight. Young birds have white on tail, with a black band near the tip.

Young bird

This gull is a formidable predator, capable of swallowing an egg or gull chick whole.

SITES GUIDE

Great black-backed gulls are less colonial than most gulls, but build a typical gull nest of piled-up plant rubbish.

The species may be seen at sites numbers: 1-6, 9-12, 19-21, 23-25, 27, 34, 41, 52, 54, 57, 58, 64.

Pink legs

Like other gulls, these birds flock around coastal fishing craft throwing out fish waste.

The great black-backed gull has a heavy bill and darker upper parts than the lesser black-backed gull. Sexes are alike. 25–31 in. (64–79 cm).

Present all year; birds from Europe also winter in Britain.

Great black-backed gull *Larus marinus*

Nothing weak enough to be overpowered and killed by the great black-backed gull is safe while this butcher of the bird world is about. With its heavy, hook-tipped bill, it feeds voraciously on anything from crabs, molluscs and worms, to fish, mice and voles. Puffins, kittiwakes, Manx shearwaters and even sickly lambs are vulnerable. The bird is also a scavenger of carrion and edible refuse thrown from ships.

Breeding, either singly or in colonies, is confined to rocky coasts where cliffs, islets and offshore stacks offer refuge from mammal predators. Both sexes build a large nest on the ground, between May and early June, using seaweed, heather, grass and a few feathers. The usual clutch is three eggs, which are a pale buff or olive-brown, blotched and speckled with dark brown and grey. The greyish chicks, mottled with black, are hatched by both parents and fledge after seven weeks' feeding.

In spite of its omnivorous nature, this bird is the rarest of Britain's indigenous gulls, although its numbers have been increasing during the last century – possibly because of the gradual warming of the North Atlantic Ocean and an increase in the quantity of fish offal and edible refuse thrown away by man.

Location	Behaviour	Sketch
Date		
Time		
Weather	Field marks	
Call		

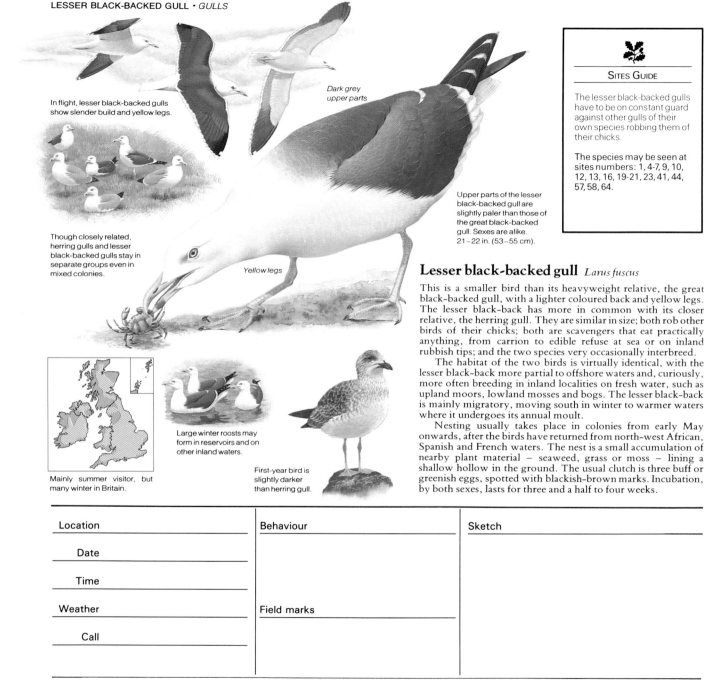

In flight, lesser black-backed gulls show slender build and yellow legs.

Though closely related, herring gulls and lesser black-backed gulls stay in separate groups even in mixed colonies.

Dark grey upper parts

Yellow legs

Upper parts of the lesser black-backed gull are slightly paler than those of the great black-backed gull. Sexes are alike. 21–22 in. (53–55 cm).

Mainly summer visitor, but many winter in Britain.

Large winter roosts may form in reservoirs and on other inland waters.

First-year bird is slightly darker than herring gull.

SITES GUIDE

The lesser black-backed gulls have to be on constant guard against other gulls of their own species robbing them of their chicks.

The species may be seen at sites numbers: 1, 4-7, 9, 10, 12, 13, 16, 19-21, 23, 41, 44, 57, 58, 64.

Lesser black-backed gull *Larus fuscus*

This is a smaller bird than its heavyweight relative, the great black-backed gull, with a lighter coloured back and yellow legs. The lesser black-back has more in common with its closer relative, the herring gull. They are similar in size; both rob other birds of their chicks; both are scavengers that eat practically anything, from carrion to edible refuse at sea or on inland rubbish tips; and the two species very occasionally interbreed.

The habitat of the two birds is virtually identical, with the lesser black-back more partial to offshore waters and, curiously, more often breeding in inland localities on fresh water, such as upland moors, lowland mosses and bogs. The lesser black-back is mainly migratory, moving south in winter to warmer waters where it undergoes its annual moult.

Nesting usually takes place in colonies from early May onwards, after the birds have returned from north-west African, Spanish and French waters. The nest is a small accumulation of nearby plant material – seaweed, grass or moss – lining a shallow hollow in the ground. The usual clutch is three buff or greenish eggs, spotted with blackish-brown marks. Incubation, by both sexes, lasts for three and a half to four weeks.

Location	Behaviour	Sketch
Date		
Time		
Weather	Field marks	
Call		

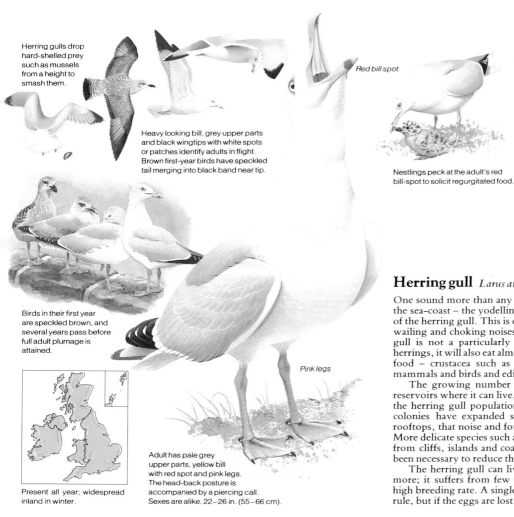

Herring gulls drop hard-shelled prey such as mussels from a height to smash them.

Heavy looking bill, grey upper parts and black wingtips with white spots or patches identify adults in flight. Brown first-year birds have speckled tail merging into black band near tip.

Red bill spot

Nestlings peck at the adult's red bill-spot to solicit regurgitated food.

Birds in their first year are speckled brown, and several years pass before full adult plumage is attained.

Pink legs

Adult has pale grey upper parts, yellow bill with red spot and pink legs. The head-back posture is accompanied by a piercing call. Sexes are alike. 22–26 in. (55–66 cm).

Present all year; widespread inland in winter.

Herring gull *Larus argentatus*

One sound more than any other conjures up the atmosphere of the sea-coast – the yodelling 'kee-owk-kyowk-kyowk-kyowk' of the herring gull. This is one of a large vocabulary of mewing, wailing and choking noises characteristic of this bird. 'Herring' gull is not a particularly apt name, for although it will eat herrings, it will also eat almost anything else, particularly animal food – crustacea such as shrimps, prawns and crabs, small mammals and birds and edible rubbish.

The growing number and size of rubbish dumps, and of reservoirs where it can live, has encouraged the great increase in the herring gull population that has recently occurred. Some colonies have expanded so much, spilling over even on to rooftops, that noise and fouling have become major problems. More delicate species such as puffins and terns have been driven from cliffs, islands and coastal dunes, so that drastic culls have been necessary to reduce the gulls' numbers.

The herring gull can live long, occasionally for 30 years or more; it suffers from few predators once mature, and it has a high breeding rate. A single clutch of three eggs in a season is the rule, but if the eggs are lost more are laid.

Location	Behaviour	Sketch
Date		
Time		
Weather	Field marks	
Call		

Shaggy crest

Black bill, yellow tip

Adult in summer plumage has a black forehead and crown, a shaggy crest and a black, yellow-tipped bill. Sexes are alike. 16 in. (41 cm). Downy chicks have a characteristic 'spiky' plumage.

Courtship behaviour includes 'fish-flight', when the male offers fish to the female in mid-air.

Adult, summer

Adult, winter

Heavy flight and dark bill are conspicuous at all seasons. In winter the forehead is white.

After fledging, young birds gather on sand-banks near the colony.

Mar.–Sept. visitor; coastal, a few nest inland in Ireland.

In courtship displays on the ground, the neck and bill are stretched upwards and the wings held out from the body.

SITES GUIDE

Some Sandwich terns start to develop winter plumage, their foreheads streaked with white, before the breeding season ends.

The species may be seen at sites numbers: 1, 9, 10, 12, 15, 19, 26, 31, 44, 53, 56, 57, 63, 64.

Sandwich tern *Sterna sandvicensis*

The surest sign that the breeding season of the sandwich tern has started is when two birds are seen conducting their 'fish-flight', in which one of the birds carries a fish. Early in the breeding season the two birds are not necessarily male and female, and either may carry the fish; but later the sexes pair off, and the male feeds its fish to its mate as part of the courtship ritual. This extra nutrient probably helps to strengthen the female while she is producing eggs.

It is in the breeding season that the terns are at their most quarrelsome, and the colonies resound with the harsh 'kirrick' that is their usual call. Both sexes incubate the eggs, for a period of three weeks. When the female is incubating, the male brings food in the form of marine worms, sand eels and other small fish. It catches these by making headlong plunges into the water. The chicks assemble with the young of other sandwich terns when one or two weeks old, but their parents are apparently able to distinguish them from the crowd. They fly at about five weeks. Juveniles lack a yellow tip to their bills.

The bird is called after the town in east Kent, the scientist who named the species having received a specimen from there.

Location	Behaviour	Sketch
Date		
Time		
Weather	Field marks	
Call		

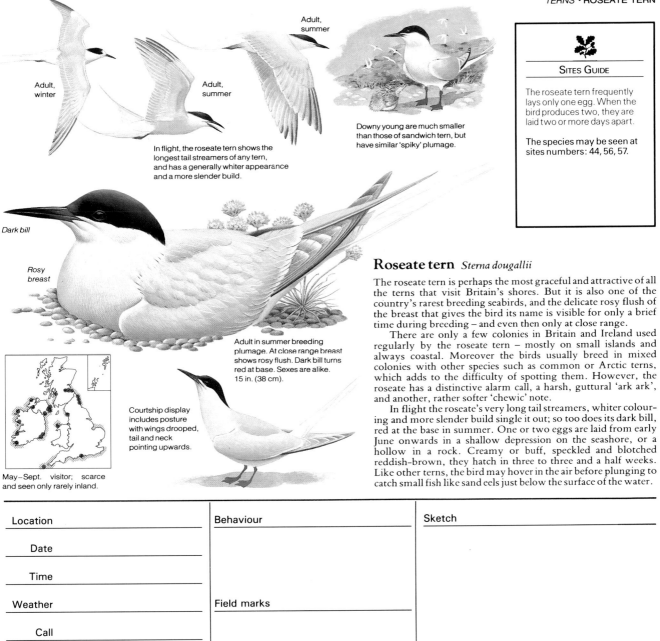

Adult, winter

Adult, summer

Adult, summer

Adult, summer

In flight, the roseate tern shows the longest tail streamers of any tern, and has a generally whiter appearance and a more slender build.

Downy young are much smaller than those of sandwich tern, but have similar 'spiky' plumage.

Dark bill

Rosy breast

Adult in summer breeding plumage. At close range breast shows rosy flush. Dark bill turns red at base. Sexes are alike. 15 in. (38 cm).

Courtship display includes posture with wings drooped, tail and neck pointing upwards.

May–Sept. visitor; scarce and seen only rarely inland.

Roseate tern *Sterna dougallii*

The roseate tern is perhaps the most graceful and attractive of all the terns that visit Britain's shores. But it is also one of the country's rarest breeding seabirds, and the delicate rosy flush of the breast that gives the bird its name is visible for only a brief time during breeding – and even then only at close range.

There are only a few colonies in Britain and Ireland used regularly by the roseate tern – mostly on small islands and always coastal. Moreover the birds usually breed in mixed colonies with other species such as common or Arctic terns, which adds to the difficulty of spotting them. However, the roseate has a distinctive alarm call, a harsh, guttural 'ark ark', and another, rather softer 'chewic' note.

In flight the roseate's very long tail streamers, whiter colouring and more slender build single it out; so too does its dark bill, red at the base in summer. One or two eggs are laid from early June onwards in a shallow depression on the seashore, or a hollow in a rock. Creamy or buff, speckled and blotched reddish-brown, they hatch in three to three and a half weeks. Like other terns, the bird may hover in the air before plunging to catch small fish like sand eels just below the surface of the water.

Location	Behaviour	Sketch
Date		
Time		
Weather	Field marks	
Call		

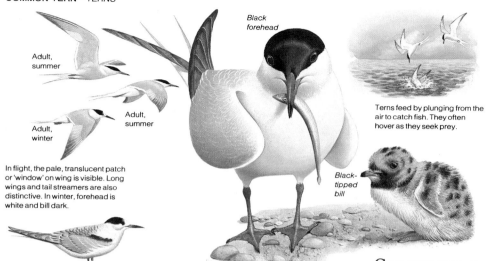

Black forehead

Adult, summer

Adult, summer

Adult, winter

In flight, the pale, translucent patch or 'window' on wing is visible. Long wings and tail streamers are also distinctive. In winter, forehead is white and bill dark.

Terns feed by plunging from the air to catch fish. They often hover as they seek prey.

Black-tipped bill

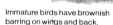

Immature birds have brownish barring on wings and back.

Adult in summer has black-tipped red bill and black forehead. Legs are fairly long. Sexes are alike. 14 in. (36 cm). Chicks are mottled and barred.

The hubbub of a ternery stops occasionally when all the birds rise in a silent, graceful cloud to sweep out over the sea for a minute or so, then return.

Apr.–Sept. visitor; also passage bird. Mainly coastal.

SITES GUIDE

Unlike the Arctic tern, the common tern often makes its nest near inland stretches of water, particularly in Scotland.

The species may be seen at sites numbers: 1-3, 9, 10, 12, 13, 15, 21, 26, 30, 31, 44, 49, 53, 56, 57, 63, 64.

Common tern *Sterna hirundo*

In spite of its name this species is not Britain's commonest tern – a distinction that belongs to the very similar and closely related Arctic tern. But it is the most widely distributed tern, breeding around much of the Irish and Scottish mainland and island coastlines, and also in southern and south-eastern England.

The common tern frequently breeds in mixed colonies with other species of tern, some colonies numbering many thousands of pairs. Visitors to the nesting area are certain to be 'dive-bombed' repeatedly; although the common tern is less inclined than the Arctic tern to press home its attack to the point of actually striking a blow, its bill does occasionally draw blood.

The nest is merely a scrape in the ground, either unlined or scattered with a few plant strands. Two to three eggs are laid from the end of May to early June. Most vary in colour from stone to brownish or yellowish, speckled and blotched with dark brown and ash-grey. The chicks hatch at intervals of one or two days and remain in the nest for several days more. During their time in the nest, the female normally broods and protects them while her mate fetches food. Common terns eat small fish, crabs and shrimps, marine worms, starfish and molluscs.

Location	Behaviour	Sketch
Date		
Time		
Weather	Field marks	
Call		

When a mixed group of Arctic and common terns is seen at a distance, the two species are scarcely distinguishable.

All-red bill

In flight, underparts always appear greyer than in common tern, and under-wing is translucent. Winter plumage is otherwise similar to common tern.

Adult, winter

Adult, summer

Adult, summer

Adult in summer plumage, recognisable by very short legs and usually all-red bill. Sexes alike. 14 in. (36 cm).

Short legs

A fox intruding into a colony comes under fierce attack. Sometimes blood is drawn from human visitors.

Other birds, such as eiders, often nest in Arctic tern colonies, protected by the terns' aggressive reaction to intruders.

Apr.–Sept. visitor; most numerous in northern isles.

Arctic tern *Sterna paradisaea*

Of all the terns that breed in Britain, the Arctic species is the most numerous, with around 50,000 pairs nesting every year. Most are concentrated in the north, few pairs breeding south of a line from the Scottish borders to Anglesey. Nearly all colonies in the British Isles are on or very near the coast. In them, Arctic terns usually mingle with common terns, adding to the problems of identifying birds that are, in any case, much alike in appearance.

Arctic terns arrive from their southern–ocean wintering grounds in May, and many clutches are complete by the end of the month. They generally consist of two eggs – occasionally one or three – which are similar to those of the common tern. Both parents tend the chicks, which at first normally remain in or very near the nest; though they can, if need be, swim when only two days old.

The call of the Arctic tern is a harsh 'kee-yaar', like that of the common tern, but with a tendency for the emphasis to fall on the second syllable. When an attack on human intruders is being pushed home the calls may become more excited, with a harsh growling 'kaar' just as the bird strikes or passes close overhead.

Location	Behaviour	Sketch
Date		
Time		
Weather	Field marks	
Call		

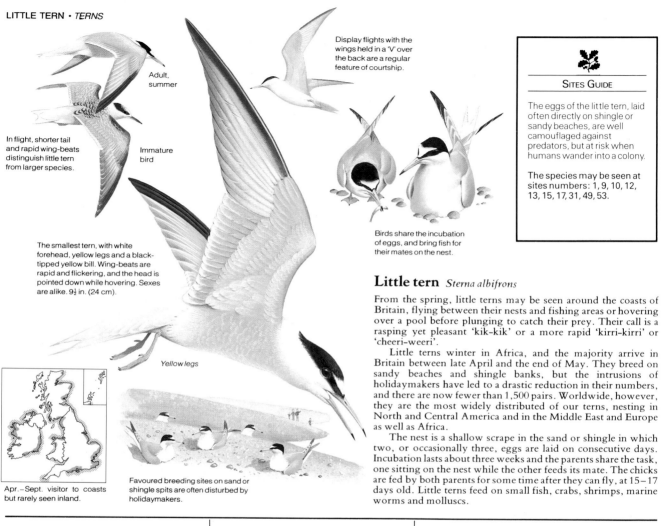

Adult, summer

Display flights with the wings held in a 'V' over the back are a regular feature of courtship.

In flight, shorter tail and rapid wing-beats distinguish little tern from larger species.

Immature bird

The smallest tern, with white forehead, yellow legs and a black-tipped yellow bill. Wing-beats are rapid and flickering, and the head is pointed down while hovering. Sexes are alike. 9½ in. (24 cm).

Yellow legs

Birds share the incubation of eggs, and bring fish for their mates on the nest.

Apr.–Sept. visitor to coasts but rarely seen inland.

Favoured breeding sites on sand or shingle spits are often disturbed by holidaymakers.

SITES GUIDE

The eggs of the little tern, laid often directly on shingle or sandy beaches, are well camouflaged against predators, but at risk when humans wander into a colony.

The species may be seen at sites numbers: 1, 9, 10, 12, 13, 15, 17, 31, 49, 53.

Little tern *Sterna albifrons*

From the spring, little terns may be seen around the coasts of Britain, flying between their nests and fishing areas or hovering over a pool before plunging to catch their prey. Their call is a rasping yet pleasant 'kik-kik' or a more rapid 'kirri-kirri' or 'cheeri-weeri'.

Little terns winter in Africa, and the majority arrive in Britain between late April and the end of May. They breed on sandy beaches and shingle banks, but the intrusions of holidaymakers have led to a drastic reduction in their numbers, and there are now fewer than 1,500 pairs. Worldwide, however, they are the most widely distributed of our terns, nesting in North and Central America and in the Middle East and Europe as well as Africa.

The nest is a shallow scrape in the sand or shingle in which two, or occasionally three, eggs are laid on consecutive days. Incubation lasts about three weeks and the parents share the task, one sitting on the nest while the other feeds its mate. The chicks are fed by both parents for some time after they can fly, at 15–17 days old. Little terns feed on small fish, crabs, shrimps, marine worms and molluscs.

Location	Behaviour	Sketch
Date		
Time		
Weather	Field marks	
Call		

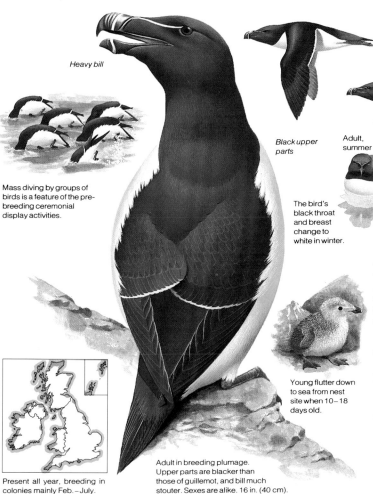

Heavy bill

Mass diving by groups of birds is a feature of the pre-breeding ceremonial display activities.

Bird rises laboriously, pattering along the surface, but then flies strongly with rapid wing-beats.

Black upper parts

Adult, summer

Adult, winter

The bird's black throat and breast change to white in winter.

Present all year, breeding in colonies mainly Feb.–July.

Young flutter down to sea from nest site when 10–18 days old.

Adult in breeding plumage. Upper parts are blacker than those of guillemot, and bill much stouter. Sexes are alike. 16 in. (40 cm).

Sites Guide

Colonies of razorbills breed in remote, sheltered crevices in cliffs or on rocky foreshores. There is no nesting material.

The species may be seen at sites numbers: 1, 4-6, 9, 12, 13, 20, 21, 23, 44, 47, 50, 52, 64, 65.

Razorbill *Alca torda*

Anyone handling a razorbill without thick gloves is liable to find out quickly how it acquired its common name. The bird's very sharp, hooked upper mandible, well suited to grasping the fish and marine invertebrates which make up its diet, also enables it to look after itself against many would-be predators.

From a greater distance, a watcher can see razorbills in 'rafts' or strings riding out the swell. In the breeding season courting couples may be striking the so-called 'ecstatic' pose, in which one bird stretches its beak upwards, emitting a grating noise with bill parted, while its mate nibbles its throat.

Razorbills tend to nest in the same areas as guillemots, but choose more protected sites. Some breeding colonies may number many thousands of birds; one, at Horn Head in County Donegal, was estimated in 1969–70 to hold 45,000 pairs. Egg laying generally begins in early May. Both adults share the incubation duties, and the feeding of the young, usually only one. The chick makes its way to the sea when about two weeks old, so continues to be tended by the parents. The journey to the water is undertaken under cover of darkness, to avoid the attentions of predatory gulls.

Location	Behaviour	Sketch
Date		
Time		
Weather	Field marks	
Call		

Slim pointed
bill

Adult in breeding
plumage. Upper parts
are paler and browner
than those of razorbill;
bill is dagger-shaped.
Sexes are alike. 16½ in.
(42 cm).

Dark brown
above

Adult in winter
plumage has white
face and breast, and
fine black line behind eye.

Newly fledged young
make their first journey
down to the sea at
dusk, to reduce danger
from predators.

SITES GUIDE

The guillemot's single egg is
elongated and tapered,
reducing the risk of it rolling
off the rock-ledge breeding
site.

The species may be seen at
sites numbers: 1, 3-6, 13, 19,
20, 23, 44, 47, 50, 52, 65.

A few guillemots are 'bridled', having
a white line behind the eye when in
breeding plumage.

Breeds Apr.–July, but some
return to colonies in winter.

A 'bowing' action is
frequently seen among
birds in a colony.

Guillemots nest in dense colonies
on precipitous cliff ledges.

Guillemot *Uria aalge*

When standing upright with its black–brown upper parts and
pure white underparts fully visible, the guillemot is the nearest
approximation to that feathered 'waiter' of Antarctic waters, the
penguin, that exists in Britain. Another similarity is the way in
which the breeding birds crowd together in vast colonies.
Guillemots need breeding sites near their marine food supply
that are as safe as possible from predators. The ledges of islands
and offshore rock pillars provide these, but space is limited and
the birds pack themselves onto whatever footholds are available,
often having just room to stand.

Like many other seabirds, guillemots congregate well before
breeding begins in late May. The single egg is strongly tapered;
probably a natural adaptation which allows it to roll in a circle on
the bare ledge on which it is laid, rather than fall off. Both sexes
incubate the egg, balancing it on their feet and covering it with
their belly plumage.

The chick is fairly helpless, and if undisturbed remains on its
ledge for four to five weeks. Then, still only partly grown, it
makes its way down to the sea, where it continues to develop
until it flies about three weeks later.

Location	Behaviour	Sketch
Date		
Time		
Weather	Field marks	
Call		

White face

Triangular bill

Flight is rapid, with whirring wing-beats.

Webbed feet are spread as 'air-brakes' when landing.

In winter the face is darker, the bill less colourful and the horny eye-patch is lost.

Chick has long brown down and small bill. Plumage develops during seven weeks in burrow.

Present all year, mainly on north and west coasts.

A portly build and massive bill, vividly coloured in summer, make adult puffins, male and female, unmistakable. In breeding plumage the face is white, with a horny patch above and below the eye. 12 in. (30 cm).

Juvenile birds have more slender bills than adults.

SITES GUIDE

Breeding colonies of puffin dig nesting burrows in grassy cliff tops. Usually only one egg is laid each year, in May.

The species may be seen at sites numbers: 5, 6, 9, 20, 21, 44, 47, 50, 52, 62, 64-66.

Puffin *Fratercula arctica*

Its huge red, blue and yellow bill and its orange feet make the puffin one of Britain's more colourful birds, and distinguish it clearly from its close but larger relatives in the auk family, the razorbill and guillemot. This distinctive bill has given the bird its popular names 'sea parrot' and 'bottlenose'.

The puffin is a marine species, and is only rarely seen inland on fresh water when driven ashore by storms. It is a good diver, and thanks to the size of its bill can catch as many as ten small fish in succession without having to swallow, carrying them cross-wise. The bird breeds in colonies sometimes numbering thousands of pairs, which nest in shallow burrows that they dig in the soft turf on cliff tops and islands, or in burrows taken over from rabbits or shearwaters. The puffin's rare call, a deep growling 'arr', is heard near its breeding sites.

Parents share incubation, and both feed the chick for about 40 days, then desert it. The chick stays in its burrow for seven to ten days, without food, as its plumage develops. It then makes its way to the sea by night to avoid hungry gulls. The young puffin does not return to the colony for two to three years, and does not breed until it is four to five years old.

Location	Behaviour	Sketch
Date		
Time		
Weather	Field marks	
Call		

Group displays include formation swimming in line astern or line abreast.

Black body

White wing-patch

Perching attitude is usually more crouched than that of the guillemot. The black guillemot seldom roves as far out to sea as other guillemots.

Summer plumage is completely dark except for white wing-patches. The posture is a pre-breeding display. Sexes are alike. 13½ in. (34 cm).

Present all year at breeding sites on north-west coasts.

Upper parts in winter are barred black and white, with the head and underparts mainly white.

Wings are used to aid underwater steering when the bird dives for fish, usually in shallow water.

Black guillemot *Cepphus grylle*

No other bird breeding in Britain can be confused with the black guillemot, for none has its uniformly black summer plumage, broken only by a prominent white wing-patch. Its red feet furnish a splash of colour in an otherwise sombrely attired bird.

The black guillemot resembles other auks in its upright stance, necessary because the legs are set far back for efficient swimming and in its pattering take-off, straight flight and rapid wing-beats, all of which are a result of the bird's small wing area in relation to its body weight. The bird's voice – a shrill and rather plaintive whistling – is, however, very different from the deep-toned barking and grunting calls of other auks. The black guillemot's call is a particular feature of the courting display, when a pair or several pairs of birds circle one another, opening their bills widely to show their bright vermilion gapes.

The black guillemot generally lays its one to three eggs in a crevice or rock-hole near the base of a cliff. The eggs are basically creamy or bluish-white, with spots of reddish-brown or black and pale grey. Incubation, lasting about 24 days, is shared, with the female apparently sitting on the eggs by day and the male taking over at night.

Location	Behaviour	Sketch
Date		
Time		
Weather	Field marks	
Call		

Adult stock dove in flight shows two short bars on each wing.

Two pairs of stock doves may fight for possession of a desirable nest-hole.

SITES GUIDE

Stock doves are social birds and tend to breed in loose colonies. They feed chiefly on stubble fields and meadows.

The species may be seen at sites numbers: 3, 11, 13, 15, 19-21, 27-29, 38, 41, 53, 57, 58.

Rock dove
Columba livia

The rock dove in flight is distinguished from the stock dove by its bolder wing-bars, its white rump and its very long wings.

Grey rump

Stock doves and rock doves present all year.

The stock dove is a smaller bird than the wood-pigeon, lacking its white neck and wing markings. Each wing has two short bars; rump is grey. Sexes are alike. 13 in. (33 cm).

Stock dove *Columba oenas*

Holes in trees and rock faces and, very occasionally, disused rabbit burrows are the stock dove's favoured nesting places. The bird is found in both coastal and inland habitats – in parkland, woodland, and farmland with old trees; and also on cliffs. The nest itself may be merely a few plant fibres, twigs or roots on the floor of the hole; sometimes there is no lining at all.

Two pure white, fairly glossy eggs are usually laid sometime between late March and July – although clutches have been recorded from the beginning of March to October. Starting with the first egg, incubation is shared by both adults and lasts for 16–18 days. The chicks, or squabs as they are called, have rather sparse, coarse tufts of yellowish-brown down. They feed on a milky secretion from the lining of the parents' crops called pigeons' milk – which they take by thrusting their bills into the adults' throats.

The birds have a distinctive display flight, with two or more doves flying in circles and loops, often with wings raised and sometimes punctuated with wing-clapping. The rock dove – similar in general appearance to the stock dove – is found mostly on the coasts of Ireland and northern and western Scotland.

Location	Behaviour	Sketch
Date		
Time		
Weather	Field marks	
Call		

Long, barred wings have dark patches at 'wrists' on both upper and lower surfaces, contrasting with the pale primary feathers.

Underparts, seen in flight, are dark at the front and pale at the rear. Tail bars are fewer but bolder than those of the long-eared owl. Sexes are alike. 15 in. (38 cm).

Pale rear

A semi-horizontal stance is often adopted when perching.

Dark front

The short-eared owl nests on the ground; the young move away before they can fly.

Present all year; more widespread in winter.

Display flight includes a loud clapping made as the wingtips meet below the body.

SITES GUIDE

The number of short-eared owls in a district depends upon the availability of short-tailed voles, their main prey.

The species may be seen at sites numbers: 12, 13, 15, 18, 28, 29, 40, 48, 51, 53.

Short-eared owl *Asio flammeus*

The short-eared owl hunts by low-level searching, its sensitive ears enabling it to pinpoint the faintest rustle in the grass as it covers rough grasslands and other open country in search of prey. The bird is immediately identified by its wing-beats which are like those of an enormous moth, the wings passing through a large arc.

The bird hunts in daylight or at dusk in treeless country, chiefly in upland Wales, the Pennines and Scotland. Some breeding pairs occur in suitable country in Kent and East Anglia.

Breeding begins from April onwards. Three to eight white eggs are laid in a shallow, unlined hollow on the ground among long grass or heather. The eggs are laid at intervals of two days or more; incubation starts with the first egg laid and lasts for 24–28 days. The chicks, clad all over in thick creamy-buff down, are fed by the female with small rodents such as short-tailed voles, and also with shrews, small birds and insects brought by the male. The short-eared owl is usually silent except when the nest is approached too closely, when a shrill 'keeorr' may be heard. The British population is joined by migrant birds from the Continent.

Location	Behaviour	Sketch
Date		
Time		
Weather	Field marks	
Call		

Richard's pipit
Anthus novaeseelandiae

This rare pipit is identifiable by its large size, long pale legs and clear eyestripe. 7 in. (18 cm).

Long hind claws

Streaked breast

In song flight, the bird flutters high into the air and then glides back to the ground. It will also sing from perches. Normal take-off flight appears weak and hesitant.

A small brown-streaked bird, stockier than tree pipit, with white outer tail feathers, brownish legs, long hind claws and a streaked breast. Sexes are alike. 5¾ in. (14·5 cm).

Juvenile

Adult

Tawny pipit
Anthus campestris

This visitor is almost unstreaked in adult plumage; the juvenile is heavily streaked. 6½ in. (16·5 cm).

Present all year, but many winter on Continent.

Meadow pipit *Anthus pratensis*

Birds which breed in open country often have conspicuous song flights, and the meadow pipit is a prime example of this. The male bird starts its performance by climbing steeply to a maximum height of 100 ft (30 m). During the ascent it utters an increasingly fast series of 'pheet' notes. These reach a climax and are replaced by slower and more liquid notes as the bird 'parachutes' down. Its outspread, upwards-pointing wings and outspread tail slow the descent. On landing, the bird rounds off its song with a trill.

At high altitudes, the meadow pipit is normally Britain's commonest song-bird. It is found from sea-level to more than 3,000 ft (900 m) and in various habitats from the Isles of Scilly to the Shetlands, and from the west of Ireland to Kent. Although its nest is usually well hidden in vegetation, it often plays host to the cuckoo. Its own eggs are usually three to five in a clutch, although six or seven are sometimes recorded in the north. The small meadow pipit is among the favourite prey of the merlin.

Richard's pipit usually arrives in small numbers from September to December. The tawny pipit is an irregular autumn visitor from continental Europe.

Location	Behaviour	Sketch
Date		
Time		
Weather	Field marks	
Call		

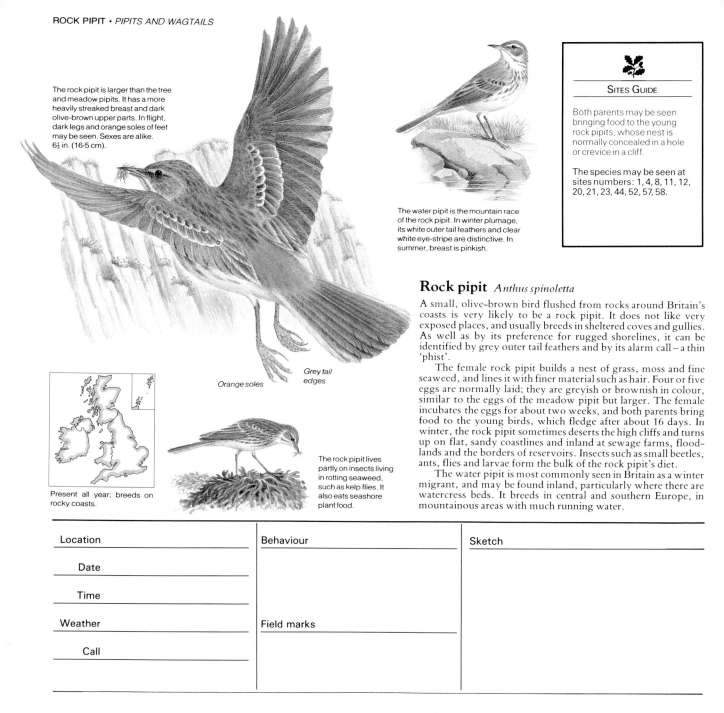

The rock pipit is larger than the tree and meadow pipits. It has a more heavily streaked breast and dark olive-brown upper parts. In flight, dark legs and orange soles of feet may be seen. Sexes are alike. 6½ in. (16·5 cm).

Grey tail edges

Orange soles

Present all year; breeds on rocky coasts.

The rock pipit lives partly on insects living in rotting seaweed, such as kelp flies. It also eats seashore plant food.

The water pipit is the mountain race of the rock pipit. In winter plumage, its white outer tail feathers and clear white eye-stripe are distinctive. In summer, breast is pinkish.

Rock pipit *Anthus spinoletta*

A small, olive-brown bird flushed from rocks around Britain's coasts is very likely to be a rock pipit. It does not like very exposed places, and usually breeds in sheltered coves and gullies. As well as by its preference for rugged shorelines, it can be identified by grey outer tail feathers and by its alarm call – a thin 'phist'.

The female rock pipit builds a nest of grass, moss and fine seaweed, and lines it with finer material such as hair. Four or five eggs are normally laid; they are greyish or brownish in colour, similar to the eggs of the meadow pipit but larger. The female incubates the eggs for about two weeks, and both parents bring food to the young birds, which fledge after about 16 days. In winter, the rock pipit sometimes deserts the high cliffs and turns up on flat, sandy coastlines and inland at sewage farms, floodlands and the borders of reservoirs. Insects such as small beetles, ants, flies and larvae form the bulk of the rock pipit's diet.

The water pipit is most commonly seen in Britain as a winter migrant, and may be found inland, particularly where there are watercress beds. It breeds in central and southern Europe, in mountainous areas with much running water.

Location	Behaviour	Sketch
Date		
Time		
Weather	Field marks	
Call		

Curved red bill

Juveniles are not as glossy as adult birds. Their bills are orange-yellow rather than red.

In flight, choughs can be distinguished from jackdaws by their upturned wing-ends and musical 'keeaar' call. They glide, dive, roll and soar above the cliffs.

Red legs

Present all year; formerly more widespread.

A bird of mountain, crag and sea cliff, the chough is easy to recognise by its glossy purple-black plumage that contrasts with red legs and red, down-curved bill. Sexes are alike. 15½ in. (39 cm).

Choughs feed in small flocks, often mixing with jackdaws.

SITES GUIDE

The chough's nesting site is a ledge or crevice in a cliff or quarry, or within a cave. The young hatch after 17-23 days of incubation.

The species may be seen at sites numbers: 20, 21, 23, 25, 62.

Chough *Pyrrhocorax pyrrhocorax*

Masters of aerobatics, choughs like to wheel and soar along the cliffs on broad, rounded wings, the tips spread out like fingers. The bird's name is pronounced 'chuff', but originally it was probably an imitation of its 'keeaar' or 'cheeow' call. Old alternative names were red-legged crow and Cornish chough or daw, 'choghe' also being an old name for the jackdaw. At one time the chough was abundant in Cornwall, and an old legend tells that King Arthur's spirit entered the bird after his death.

Although once widespread in Scotland, the north of England and the south coast, the chough is now found only on a few western coasts. A succession of cold winters during the 19th century may have started its decline. Birds begin breeding from late April, building a large, cupped nest of sticks bound with other plant stems and grass and well lined with wool or hair. The three or four eggs, pale greenish or creamy in colour and finely speckled with brown and grey, are incubated by the female. Both parents regurgitate food for the young.

The chough's down-curved bill is ideally suited for its diet of worms, caterpillars, ants and other insects such as beetles, particularly dung beetles. It also eats small shellfish.

Location	Behaviour	Sketch
Date		
Time		
Weather	Field marks	
Call		

Jackdaws sometimes hover in the air showing darkish bands under wings, and dark grey tail.

Grey nape

Dark grey underparts

Birds flock together, and have a liking for derelict buildings.

This small member of the crow family is easily identified by its grey nape and dark grey underparts. Other plumage is black. Sexes are alike. 13 in. (33 cm).

A jackdaw nesting in a chimneypot can be an unwelcome visitor; after years of use, the nest sticks may block the chimney.

Jackdaw *Corvus monedula*

The thieving habits of the jackdaw were celebrated by the early 19th-century humorous poet Richard Harris Barham in *The Jackdaw of Rheims*. In the poem the bird – the most notorious robber in the crow family – steals the ring of the Cardinal Lord Archbishop of Rheims. 'The Devil,' wrote Barham, 'must be in that little Jackdaw.' Apart from snatching and hiding such inedible objects, the jackdaw occasionally steals young birds and eggs which it adds to its diet of seeds, fruit, insects and carrion.

As well as nesting in holes and chimneys, the jackdaw sometimes takes over the old nests of other birds, and occasionally even makes its nest in a rabbit burrow. The amount of nest material used depends very much upon the site. A large, exposed nest is usually lined with hair, fur, grass and wool – which the jackdaw sometimes plucks from the backs of sheep.

Late April sees the start of the breeding season, and three to seven eggs with black and grey speckles are laid. Incubation is by the female who is fed on the nest by the male. The young hatch in 17–18 days and are ready to fledge when about one month old. Usually, the jackdaw's call is a loud, explosive 'tchack'; occasionally this is expanded into a 'tchackertchack'.

Present all year; winter immigrants from Continent.

A hole in a tree trunk is a favourite nesting place.

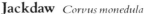

The jackdaw is a sociable bird, which often feeds with birds of other species.

Location	Behaviour	Sketch
Date		
Time		
Weather	Field marks	
Call		

Carrion, such as small mammals, form a major part of the raven's food. Occasionally it will feed on dead sheep and lambs.

When the raven croaks, the feathers on its crown and shaggy throat are raised.

Present all year; rare outside breeding range.

Adult raven is all black, with a stout, heavy bill. Its larger size, shaggy throat feathers and deeper call distinguish it from the carrion crow. Sexes are alike. 25 in. (64 cm).

Stout bill

Shaggy throat feathers

Ravens fly higher than crows, often soaring or performing aerobatics. The heavy head, extended neck and diamond-shaped tail are prominent.

SITES GUIDE

Occasionally the raven will nest in a tree, but it usually chooses a sheltered, rocky ledge in a crag or cliff.

The species may be seen at sites numbers: 4-8, 11, 20-25, 27, 28, 35-42, 48, 51, 52, 54, 62.

Raven *Corvus corax*

For centuries the raven was regarded as a bird of ill-omen and a harbinger of death, probably because of its dark colouring and its habit of feeding on the corpses of victims of the gibbet. It was once common in Britain, but years of persecution by man have driven it to mountainous regions, and to cliffs, quarries, moors and windswept hills. The largest member of the crow family, renowned for its intelligence, the raven is also the largest species of perching bird in the world.

Ravens raise only one brood each year, starting very early in the spring, in February or March. Both sexes build the large nest of twigs, sticks, heather stalks and sometimes pieces of seaweed. It is reinforced with earth and moss, and the cup is thickly lined with grass, moss and an inner layer of hair and wool. There are usually four to six eggs, light blue or green with greyish or blackish-brown speckling. The male feeds the female on the nest while she incubates the eggs, which hatch in about three weeks. The chicks are five to six weeks old before they can fly.

Ravens have a varied diet. As well as eating carrion they kill their own prey – birds or small mammals such as meadow pipits or rabbits – and forage for eggs, reptiles, insects and seeds.

Location	Behaviour	Sketch
Date		
Time		
Weather	Field marks	
Call		

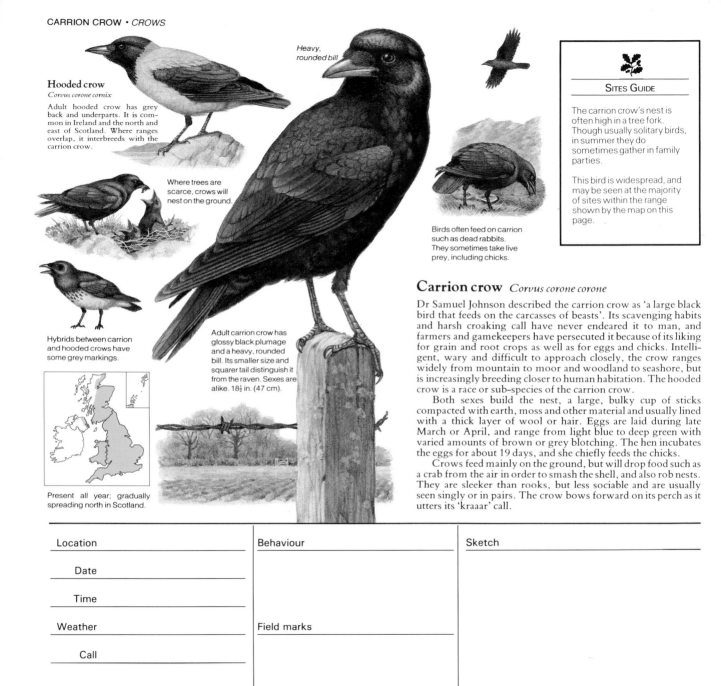

Hooded crow
Corvus corone cornix
Adult hooded crow has grey back and underparts. It is common in Ireland and the north and east of Scotland. Where ranges overlap, it interbreeds with the carrion crow.

Where trees are scarce, crows will nest on the ground.

Hybrids between carrion and hooded crows have some grey markings.

Present all year; gradually spreading north in Scotland.

Adult carrion crow has glossy black plumage and a heavy, rounded bill. Its smaller size and squarer tail distinguish it from the raven. Sexes are alike. 18½ in. (47 cm).

Heavy, rounded bill

Birds often feed on carrion such as dead rabbits. They sometimes take live prey, including chicks.

SITES GUIDE

The carrion crow's nest is often high in a tree fork. Though usually solitary birds, in summer they do sometimes gather in family parties.

This bird is widespread, and may be seen at the majority of sites within the range shown by the map on this page.

Carrion crow *Corvus corone corone*

Dr Samuel Johnson described the carrion crow as 'a large black bird that feeds on the carcasses of beasts'. Its scavenging habits and harsh croaking call have never endeared it to man, and farmers and gamekeepers have persecuted it because of its liking for grain and root crops as well as for eggs and chicks. Intelligent, wary and difficult to approach closely, the crow ranges widely from mountain to moor and woodland to seashore, but is increasingly breeding closer to human habitation. The hooded crow is a race or sub-species of the carrion crow.

Both sexes build the nest, a large, bulky cup of sticks compacted with earth, moss and other material and usually lined with a thick layer of wool or hair. Eggs are laid during late March or April, and range from light blue to deep green with varied amounts of brown or grey blotching. The hen incubates the eggs for about 19 days, and she chiefly feeds the chicks.

Crows feed mainly on the ground, but will drop food such as a crab from the air in order to smash the shell, and also rob nests. They are sleeker than rooks, but less sociable and are usually seen singly or in pairs. The crow bows forward on its perch as it utters its 'kraaar' call.

Location	Behaviour	Sketch
Date		
Time		
Weather	Field marks	
Call		

Young birds lack the contrasting plumage of adults. They are grey-brown above, speckled white below.

Flight is direct and fast on whirring, short wings.

Dippers often prefer swimming to flying.

Short tail

Often seen perched on a boulder in a stream, the adult dipper has dark upper parts, white throat and breast and a chestnut waistband. Short tail and constant bobbing habit make it unmistakable. Sexes are alike. 7 in. (18 cm).

Present all year; some continental birds in winter.

The dipper has the remarkable ability to walk underwater up the beds of fast-flowing streams in search of food; it also dives into water from the air.

Continental black-bellied form, without chestnut band, occasionally appears in winter.

Sites Guide

The dipper's young are fed by both birds. The nest is often found under a bridge or the overhang of a river bank, or behind a waterfall.

The species may be seen at sites numbers: 8, 11, 22, 28, 29, 32, 34-36, 39-41, 48, 51.

Dipper *Cinclus cinclus*

In contrast to all other birds, the dipper seeks its food by walking underwater on shallow river beds and the bottoms of streams. With its head down in search of water insects, tadpoles and worms, it may forge its way against the current, kept on its feet, probably, by the force of water pressing down on its broad back. Before submerging, the dipper often perches on rocks in the middle of rushing, tumbling water and repeatedly bobs up and down. Its legs flex, its wings quiver, its white eyelids blink, and its sweet, warbling song – which it maintains for most of the year – can be heard above the noise of the water.

The dipper is a plump, wren-like bird, with a distinctive, snow-white breast. Because of its feeding habits, it is mostly found in the uplands of western, central and northern Britain, where there are fast-running streams.

The bird's low, rapid and direct flight usually follows the course of a river; and it often spends the entire year on the same stretch of water. Dippers can swim on or under water. The bulky, domed nest is built of moss, and the white eggs, usually five, are laid in late March. Nestlings hatch in 15–18 days and fly after about three weeks. They can swim even earlier.

Location	Behaviour	Sketch
Date		
Time		
Weather	Field marks	
Call		

Cocked tail

The wren has a distinctive, whirring flight on its short, rounded wings. Its flight is fast and direct.

Any suitable nest site may be chosen, such as an undisturbed object in a garden shed.

The wren's loud, explosive 'tit-tit-tit' song is delivered from exposed places, often from rocks or walls.

Present all year; widespread throughout British Isles.

Although busy and energetic, the wren is elusive outside the breeding season. Usually it shows itself only for a moment while flitting from one thicket to another in its search for food.

The adult bird's short, cocked tail is distinctive. Plumage is reddish-brown. The wren feeds on insects and small seeds. Sexes are alike. 3¾ in. (9·5 cm).

Wren *Troglodytes troglodytes*

Hard winters deny food to the wren, along with many other species, and because of its tiny size the wren chills much more rapidly than larger birds. In freezing weather, therefore, massive mortality may occur, as in early 1963. After a spell of mild winters has enabled it to multiply, however, the wren becomes Britain's most numerous breeding bird. It is found throughout the British Isles from Shetland to the Scillies, and from the Atlantic islands off County Kerry to Kent.

Although tiny, inconspicuous and skulking, wrens are not difficult to locate, at least when in full voice between February and July. Then the song is shrill, and delivered with much force. It consists of a rattling warble of clear notes that lasts about five seconds, and is repeated at intervals.

The male bird builds a number of ball-shaped nests, made of leaves, dried grass and moss, with an entrance at the side near the top. They are sited in hedges, ivy-covered walls, tree trunks, outbuildings, and even in the old nests of other birds. The hen bird chooses one nest, and lines it plentifully with feathers. There are normally five to eight eggs, white in colour and speckled with black or reddish-brown at the larger end.

Location	Behaviour	Sketch
Date		
Time		
Weather	Field marks	
Call		

Spot above bill

Juvenile is speckled, like young spotted flycatcher, but has white wing-patches.

Pied flycatchers glean prey such as caterpillars from tree foliage, as well as catching insects in flight.

Wing-patch

Male, summer

Female, summer

Adult male is black above and white below, with a white wing-patch and a white spot above the bill. 5 in. (12·5 cm).

Adult female is distinguished from male by grey-brown upper plumage and lack of white spot above the bill.

Present Apr.–Oct.; passage migrants in autumn.

After catching an insect, the pied flycatcher often takes its prey to the ground.

Sites Guide

The pied flycatcher is always on the lookout for insects; but after darting out in attack, seldom returns to the same perch.

The species may be seen at sites numbers: 1, 9, 11, 22, 25, 27-29, 35, 41, 57.

Pied flycatcher *Ficedula hypoleuca*

During the last 40 years or so, the pied flycatcher has extended its breeding range from Wales to the valleys and foothills of upland England. This increase may have been assisted by the deliberate provision of nest-boxes by bird lovers in some areas. The bird is also found to a lesser extent in the Pennines, southern Scotland and the Scottish Highlands; but it is not seen at all in Ireland. Unlike the spotted flycatcher, male and female have different breeding plumage, although in autumn the male's black upper parts dull to the female's grey-brown colour.

The pied flycatcher needs a plentiful supply of caterpillars and other insects on which to feed. Tree-stumps and dead branches provide ideal song posts and holes for nesting. The nest site is chosen by the male when he arrives from Africa in the spring. The female follows a little later and builds the nest. She lines it with animal hair, wool and feathers.

The single, annual clutch usually consists of four to seven eggs. They are pale blue, and very occasionally have a few extremely fine, reddish–brown speckles. The male feeds the female while she is incubating the eggs, which takes just under a fortnight. The young can fly after about two weeks.

Location	Behaviour	Sketch
Date		
Time		
Weather	Field marks	
Call		

The wheatear often chases insects upwards in vertical flight, with fluttering wing-beats.

Adult female is brown with buff underparts, but has the same tail pattern as the male.

White rump

Grey above

Black cheeks

Adult male in summer has grey upper parts, black cheeks and wings, white rump and black, inverted-T tail pattern. In autumn he resembles the female. 6 in. (15 cm).

Juvenile bird is brown like adult female, but also heavily speckled.

Mar.–Oct. visitor, and also passage migrant.

In flight, white rump and black, T-shaped tail pattern are conspicuous.

When the wheatears arrive, usually in March, they can be seen seeking insects, larvae and centipedes in ploughed fields.

SITES GUIDE

Wheatear nests are built under stones or in crevices. Both parents feed the dark grey nestlings with insects.

The species may be seen at sites numbers: 4, 8, 11-13, 22-25, 27-29, 32, 34, 35, 37-41, 47, 48, 52, 54.

Wheatear *Oenanthe oenanthe*

One of the first signs that spring is on its way is the arrival in Britain of the wheatear, among the earliest of the summer migrants. Normally, early arrivals from Africa are seen in southern England about the second week in March; most birds appear between the last week of March and mid-April.

The most noticeable feature of the wheatear is its white rump, visible as the bird flits low over the ground to perch on a prominent stone, clod of earth or other vantage point. The bird's common name comes from *hwit* and *oers*, Anglo-Saxon words for 'white' and 'rump'.

The wheatear is mainly a bird of upland Britain, and elsewhere occurs mostly on heathlands and coasts. It is in such areas that suitable nest sites in the form of holes in drystone walls or under large stones are most plentiful. The nest of loose grass, stems and leaves is built largely by the female. The four to seven pale blue eggs are laid in late March, or as late as June in the north. They hatch after 14 days and the young spend about two weeks in the nest. The wheatear is noted for its distinctive 'wee-chat-chat' call; its song is a vigorous, though brief, warble, intermingled with harsh rattlings and squeaky notes.

Location	Behaviour	Sketch
Date		
Time		
Weather	Field marks	
Call		

Adult male is sooty black, with a white wing-patch and rust-coloured tail. 5½ in. (14 cm).

White patch

Rusty tail

Wing-patches show prominently when the bird hovers to catch its insect prey.

Adult female is less black than the male, and lacks the white wing-patch.

The juvenile bird has speckled plumage but is otherwise similar to the adult female.

Small numbers breed; a few winter in south.

Migrating birds are often seen on rocky beaches. They can be distinguished from redstarts by darker breasts and greyer upper parts.

SITES GUIDE

For black redstarts, breeding begins in late April. Nests, in crevices, are usually made of grass, moss and roots, lined with feathers.

The species may be seen at sites numbers: 11, 13, 38.

Black redstart *Phoenicurus ochruros*

Until the Second World War, black redstarts were rare breeding birds in Britain. The rubble and broken walls of bombed sites, however, provided an environment similar to the rock-falls, screes and boulder-strewn hillsides which are the birds' natural habitat on the Continent, and their numbers increased considerably. Now, an average of 30 pairs breed in Britain each year. As bomb damage was repaired after the war, some black redstarts moved to other nesting places, such as factory sites, gasworks and railway yards. Others occupy coastal cliffs.

The nest, normally built by the female alone, is a loose cup of dried grass, moss or rootlets, lined with hair, wool or feathers. It is built on a ledge or in a wall where a brick is missing, or in some other crevice; hollow trees are also sometimes used. The clutch of four to six white eggs is incubated for 12–16 days by the female, and young birds remain in the nest for 16–18 days. Often the female produces two broods, and occasionally three. The male helps with feeding, bringing beakfuls of insects.

The black redstart's song is distinctive: a fairly loud, brief, reedy warble, which can sometimes be heard from rooftops above the din of traffic.

Location	Behaviour	Sketch
Date		
Time		
Weather	Field marks	
Call		

White crescent

In flight, adult males can be distinguished by the pale edges of the flight feathers and by the white throat crescent.

Adult female is a browner grey than the male, and the crescent at the throat is less clearly marked.

Juvenile lacks the white throat crescent of the adult. It resembles a young blackbird, but is more spotted.

Mar.–Oct. visitor; also a passage migrant.

Adult male has sooty black plumage, a white crescent at the throat, and pale wing-patches. In summer it is a bird of the uplands. 9½ in. (24 cm).

During their autumn migration, ring ouzels are often gregarious, and can be found together feeding on elderberries.

SITES GUIDE

The ring ouzel nests in a tree if one is available, but on open moors it may nest in a sheltered spot on the ground.

The species may be seen at sites numbers: 11-13, 21, 22, 24, 25, 28, 29, 32-34, 36-40, 48, 54, 55.

Ring ouzel *Turdus torquatus*

It can be as well for humans – and for predatory birds – to keep away from the nest of the ring ouzel at nesting time. It is then that this normally shy and nervous bird may become aggressive. It will vigorously defend its nest against such intruders as crows or buzzards, and some individuals will strike at the head of a human being who poses a threat.

The nest, built by male and female, is much like that of the ring ouzel's close relative the blackbird; it lacks an inner mud cup, though earth is sometimes used in the foundations. Heather from the bird's upland habitat is frequently used in the nest's construction. The eggs, numbering from three to five, are normally bluish-green with bold, reddish-brown blotches. They are incubated in turn by both parents for 13–14 days. The young are fed in the nest for about another fortnight with worms, flies, caterpillars and the like. Occasionally two broods are raised in one season.

Ring ouzels are mostly seen perched on far-off rocks. When disturbed they give a loud, rattling chatter of alarm; another call is a clear, shrill 'pee-u'. Most of the birds are migratory, and start to leave the breeding grounds in late summer.

Location	Behaviour	Sketch
Date		
Time		
Weather	Field marks	
Call		

Noisy scuffles are common among flocks of fieldfares as they feed.

Fieldfares feeding on pastures often mingle with redwings and golden plovers.

Chestnut back

Grey head

In flight, fieldfares look pale in colour from below; flashes of white appear beneath the beating wings.

Adult fieldfare has a grey head and rump, chestnut back, black tail and spotted underparts. Birds are fond of windfall apples. Sexes are alike. 10 in. (25 cm).

The fieldfare rises into the air almost vertically. The unmistakable grey rump contrasts with the black tail.

Oct.–Apr. visitor; has begun to nest in Scotland.

Fieldfare *Turdus pilaris*

Large, loose flocks of fieldfares are a common feature of the winter landscape in Britain. They are noisy, clamorous birds often seen in pastures searching for seeds and small creatures such as spiders or centipedes, or on thick hawthorns attacking the bright red berries. Alternatively they may be seen flying overhead, sometimes in large flocks on their way to a communal roost, when their chattering 'chack–chack–chack' and occasional squeaking 'wccck' calls may be heard.

Both fieldfares and redwings are northern species of thrush. Few breed in this country, but large numbers arrive in autumn to spend the winter in a less severe climate than that of their native land.

Fieldfares nest in a variety of British habitats, including farmland, woodland edges, forestry plantations and moorland valleys. The breeding season depends on the latitude, starting in April in the south of the bird's range and as late as June in the north. Two clutches of five to six eggs are laid each year. The eggs, which are glossy and light blue, with reddish-brown speckles, are incubated by the female. For their 12–16 days in the nest the chicks are fed by both adults.

Location	Behaviour	Sketch
Date		
Time		
Weather	Field marks	
Call		

The crested tit, like the coal tit and treecreeper, moves along tree trunks picking insects from the bark.

Its pointed, black and white crest readily identifies this small bird. Sexes are alike. 4½ in. (12 cm).

Present all year; confined to Scottish pine woods.

Crest

Pine forests are a favourite habitat, though the birds may also be found in mixed woodland.

SITES GUIDE

In their first weeks of life the young crested tits in their tree-hole nest are fed by the male bird alone; later, both parents bring food.

The species may be seen at sites numbers: 53, 55.

Crested tit *Parus cristatus*

A distinctive soft, rattling trill in the tree canopy of pine forest or mixed woodland gives away the presence of a flock of crested tits. But the call is not heard outside a relatively small area of the central Scottish Highlands, focused on the Spey Valley. For a species which frequents so much of Europe from Spain and Greece north to central Scandinavia, it is remarkable that the crested tit is absent from such large areas of apparently suitable habitat in the British Isles.

Since the crested tit is a very sedentary species, the lack of suitable food in winter may be a crucial factor in restricting its range and preventing it from colonising the enormous areas of new pine plantation that have been established in Britain.

The nest is usually built in a hole in a tree stump excavated by the female. It is a cup of moss and lichen lined with hair, wool and sometimes spiders' webs. A clutch may vary in size from four to eight eggs, or occasionally more. They are white, speckled with various shades of red or reddish-brown, and are incubated by the female for two to two and a half weeks before they hatch. The bird's diet consists of insects and their larvae, as well as pine seeds and berries.

Location	Behaviour	Sketch
Date		
Time		
Weather	Field marks	
Call		

In flight, the male twite shows its pink rump and notched tail. The flight is fast and undulating.

Pink rump

Adult male has nondescript, streaky brown plumage, except for buff throat and pink rump. Paler wing areas resemble wing-bar of linnet, but are far less distinct. 5¼ in. (13·5 cm).

Female twite is drabber than male, with greyish rump. Her darker, unstriped throat distinguishes her from the female linnet.

Mainly resident; but some winter on coasts.

In winter, twites mix with other finches, such as linnets and greenfinches, but can be identified by their all-brown plumage.

Twite *Acanthis flavirostris*

According to some ornithologists, the name twite comes from the bird's nasal call note which sounds rather like 'twa–it'. The song, heard on the breeding-ground, is a pleasant twittering. It is similar to the somewhat faster song of the linnet, but has a more metallic and resonant quality. The twite breeds on moorland edges, rough pastures and bracken-clad hillsides; but in winter it deserts the high ground for stubble fields, salt-marshes and coastal areas where it is usually seen in flocks feeding on or near the ground. Its food is mainly vegetable matter such as weed seeds, and it will also eat insects.

Breeding is also a social affair, and the nests are often in loose-knit colonies. They are built by the females, with the males in attendance. Clutches of usually five or six eggs are laid in April or May. They are pale blue with a variety of purple, red-brown, pink or lilac speckles and spots, which are mainly grouped on the larger end.

Incubation is carried out by the female and lasts for 12 or 13 days. Both parents provide food by regurgitation, and after 15 days of parental attention the chicks leave the nest. They remain dependent for a further two weeks.

Location	Behaviour	Sketch
Date		
Time		
Weather	Field marks	
Call		

Almost entirely white wings of the adult male are unmistakable in flight.

White head

Black back

Pairs of snow buntings usually nest in a cranny between rocks. The nest is made of moss and grasses, and is sometimes lined with wool, fur or feathers.

Adult male has black and white plumage in summer. 6½ in. (16·5 cm).

Chiefly winter visitor, but a few breed on Scottish mountains.

In winter, male birds' black and white plumage is replaced by brown on back and head, with red-brown patches on head and breast and white on underparts.

Female bird is brown and white in summer, and has less white on its wings than the male.

SITES GUIDE

Snow buntings flock together in winter, and large numbers can sometimes be seen feeding on the seashore.

The species may be seen at sites numbers: 11-13, 17, 21, 25, 38, 39, 40, 51, 55, 65.

Snow bunting *Plectrophenax nivalis*

Only a small number of snow buntings have been seen nesting in Britain since the first to breed there was recorded in Scotland in 1886. The species usually breeds in the Arctic, further north than any other perching bird; but summers there are very fleeting, and so the snow bunting visits Britain between September and April to enjoy the milder climate. Even in Britain the bird does not forsake the snowy regions after which it is named, but lives on high mountains such as the Cairngorms.

The snow bunting delivers its song – a brief, fluting 'turee-turee-turee-turiwee' – either in flight or from the ground. During courtship the male sometimes displays with its song flight, rising 20–30 ft (6–9 m) into the air; at other times it walks away from the female with wings and tail spread, showing off its prominent back, wings and tail patterns. Then it turns round and runs back before repeating the performance.

Fine materials such as hair, wool and feathers line the grassy nest, which is usually concealed in a crevice or amongst rocky scree. The bird lays from four to six eggs, pale blue and speckled with brown. It feeds on insects for the most part, but in autumn and winter the diet is supplemented by reeds.

Location	Behaviour	Sketch
Date		
Time		
Weather	Field marks	
Call		

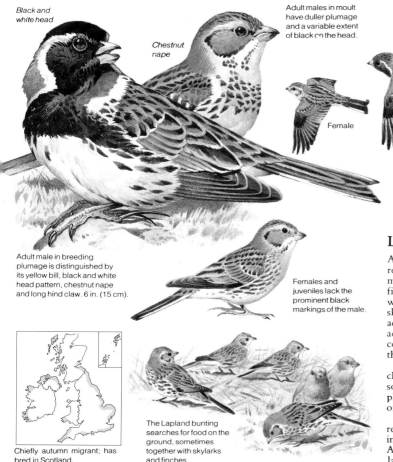

Black and white head

Chestnut nape

Adult males in moult have duller plumage and a variable extent of black on the head.

Female

Male

Male

In flight the Lapland bunting may be identified by its chestnut nape, but more often by its call of 'ticky-tick-teu'.

Adult male in breeding plumage is distinguished by its yellow bill, black and white head pattern, chestnut nape and long hind claw. 6 in. (15 cm).

Females and juveniles lack the prominent black markings of the male.

Chiefly autumn migrant; has bred in Scotland.

The Lapland bunting searches for food on the ground, sometimes together with skylarks and finches.

Lapland bunting *Calcarius lapponicus*

A brownish, sparrow–sized little bird looking rather like a hen reed bunting, seen busily running about stubble fields and marshes near the eastern coast of England with skylarks and finches, may well be a Lapland bunting. It is hunting for its winter food, the seeds of grasses and other plants. Like the skylark, it has a long claw on its hind toe – probably an adaptation to spending so much time on the ground – and this accounts for its North American name of Lapland longspur. In common with many of its relatives, such as the snow bunting, the Lapland bunting also roosts on the ground.

In summer, Lapland buntings breed in more northerly climes; most birds seen in Britain are on autumn migration, some of them staying for the winter. The handsome spring plumage of the male is not, therefore, often seen. The call most often heard in autumn is a musical 'ticky–tick–teu'.

Although in summer the Lapland bunting is found in the region after which it is named, it also occurs much further south in Norway and Sweden, and ranges east and west from Arctic Asia to Greenland and Canada. It nests in creeping birch scrub-land and marshes in open tundra.

Location	Behaviour	Sketch
Date		
Time		
Weather	Field marks	
Call		

54

53
□ Inverness

52•

55

□ Aberdeen

51

48
50
49
□ Glasgow   47
Edinburgh   45   44

46   43

59

Lough
Neagh

58
Belfast 57

□ Newcastle-upon-Tyne

40   42
39   41
36   38
35   37

34
Aire
□ Leeds

66

56

Manchester   33
32
29

□ Kingston upon Hull

26

25
Bangor
24

31
Norwich □

Dublin □
65

23

28   27
Severn   □ Birmingham

Gt Ouse

Shannon

21

22

30

London □

Suir

Blackwater   64
Cork □   63

62
61

20
19   Cardiff □   □ Bristol

18
17
16

60

12

11

Southampton □   14
10   13   15

7   Exeter □
5   6
8

3   4
2   □ Truro
1

9

0   50

MILES

The Sites

A descriptive gazetteer of places around Britain to see the birds on pages 12-95.

Order

The sites are featured in a special order, designed for ease of reference. They follow each other in a sequence determined by the Ordnance Survey's grid reference system, which works from west to east, and from south to north. The first sites described are those in Cornwall, in other words those furthest west and furthest south; the last sites described on mainland Britain are in north-east Scotland; Ulster and the Republic of Ireland are listed separately at the end.

For additional ease of reference, the sites are, however, grouped in regions and counties, and this framework takes precedence over the order required by the grid system; so that, for example, all the sites in Wales, from south to north, are listed together; then the list continues, starting afresh with the south-west corner of the Midlands, ie Gloucestershire.

Location of sites

Each site is described in terms of access from a nearby major road or town, or other major landmark. In England, Scotland and Wales, the number of the Ordnance Survey Landranger sheet (scale 1:50 000) on which the site occurs is also given, together with a grid reference number for exact and speedy location of the site on the map. Full directions on how to read a numerical grid reference are given on all Landranger sheets. Six-figure grid reference numbers are accurate to the nearest hundred metres and these are given where possible; however, it is sometimes more appropriate to quote a four-figure grid reference, accurate to the nearest kilometre, when a large area is in question. A quality motoring map will, in most cases, be adequate to locate a given site generally. The larger scale Landranger mapping is invaluable once you have arrived, for it shows public footpaths and details which enable the user to make the most of a given area.

Bird names in bold type

Bird names in **bold** are those which are featured in the identification section, pages 12-95.

Ornithological terms

A glossary explaining the meaning of ornithological terms is on pages 122-23.

1 Lizard Peninsula
2 Hayle Estuary
3 Rosemergy and Trevean Cliffs
4 Godrevy to Portreath
5 Pentire Head and Portquin Bay
6 Willapark, Tintagel
7 Crackington Haven
8 Hentor, Willings Wall and Trowlesworthy Warrens
9 Portland Bill
10 Brownsea Island
11 Holnicote Estate
12 Middle Hope and Sand Point
13 Newtown Estuary
14 East Head
15 Pagham Harbour
16 Bockhill Farm
17 Sandwich Bay
18 Shell Ness
19 Worm's Head to Port-Eynon
20 Stackpole
21 St David's Peninsula
22 Brecon Beacons

23 Lleyn Peninsula
24 The Migneint
25 Carneddau
26 Cemlyn
27 Clent Hills
28 Long Mynd
29 Longshaw
30 Northey Island and the Blackwater Estuary
31 Blakeney and Morston
32 High Peak Estate
33 Marsden Moor
34 Malham Tarn Estate
35 Eskdale
36 Wasdale
37 Scafell Group
38 Lord Lonsdale's Commons
39 Ennerdale
40 Derwentwater and Borrowdale
41 Gowbarrow and Glencoyne
42 Great Mell Fell
43 Solway Commons
44 Farne Islands
45 Lindisfarne (Holy Island)

46 Caerlaverock
47 St Abb's Head
48 Argyll Forest Park
49 Aberlady Bay
50 Bass Rock
51 Glen Coe
52 Isle of Rhum
53 Culbin Bar
54 Inverpolly
55 Cairngorms
56 Blockhouse Island and Green Island
57 Strangford Lough
58 Lighthouse Island
59 Bar Mouth
60 Cape Clear Observatory
61 Little Skellig
62 Puffin Island
63 Wexford Slobs
64 South Wexford
65 Dublin Bay area
66 Illanmaster

THE SOUTH WEST

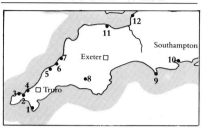

CORNWALL

1 The Lizard Peninsula

LOCATION On Cornwall's south coast, principal access from the A3083 and B3293. *Landranger Sheets 203 and 204, SW 61/71.*

The two main areas of interest on The Lizard are Mullion Island on the western side (Sheet 203, 666179) and Bass Point at the extreme southern tip (Sheet 204, 716119). Mullion Island is an important sea-bird colony, and though it is inaccessible without a boat, the many gulls and auks that breed there can be clearly seen from Mullion Cove 200 yards or so away. A few birds also breed on the mainland cliffs.

Bass Point looks out to the south and east, and is best visited during either spring or autumn when migrant birds can be seen offshore.

Highlights
Rarities in passage off Bass Point.

Time and season
Spring visits are most rewarding, since there are opportunities to see both migrant and breeding birds. All year: **fulmar, cormorant, shag, great** and **lesser black-backed gulls, kittiwake, guillemot, razorbill, jackdaw, meadow pipit, rock pipit.** Spring and autumn: migrants including **shearwaters, skuas, gannets, terns,** and **gulls.**

2 Hayle Estuary

LOCATION To the west of Hayle, in places less than half-a-mile (1 km) from the town centre. *Landranger Sheet 203, 546363.*

The small size of this estuary means that you are never far away from the birdlife feeding in the mud or bobbing on the waves, even at low tide. Many of the commoner species of waterbird are here in abundance, and there is also a chance in autumn and winter to see rare vagrants from America. There is an RSPB hide and information hut, and the path running close to the water provides an excellent vantage point.

Highlights
Terns diving for fish; rare migrants, from the continent in summer, and from the US in winter.

Time and season
Views from the hide best within two hours of high water. All year: **herring gull, common gull, great black-backed gull, redshank, oyster-catcher, dunlin.** Winter: **Slavonian grebe, long-tailed duck, black-throated diver, red-throated diver, red-breasted merganser, shelduck, turnstone, curlew, golden plover.** Spring: **shelduck, golden plover.** Summer: **terns, little stint.** Autumn: **golden plover, shelduck, wigeon, little stint.**

3 Rosemergy and Trevean Cliffs

LOCATION About 6 miles (10 km) south-west of St Ives north of the Land's End road, close to the village of Rosemergy. *Landranger Sheet 203, 415365.*

The north-facing Cornwall coast forms high cliffs at this point, either sheer or near-vertical, and topped by a narrow strip of flat land. Nesting sea-birds are the chief interest: access is easiest via Portmoina Cove. Away from the coast moorland rises to over 600 feet (200 m), so a few land-birds including birds of prey are also to be seen.

Highlights
Gulls and auks nesting.

Time and season
Best for auks and **kittiwakes** during breeding season. All year: **fulmar, gannet, shag, buzzard, kestrel, great black-backed gull, herring gull, stock dove, carrion crow, jackdaw, wren, meadow pipit.** Spring and summer: **kittiwake, guillemot, common tern.**

4 Godrevy to Portreath

LOCATION Coastland north of the B3301 coast road linking Hayle and

Redruth. *Landranger Sheet 203, 600430.*

The sea-cliffs are sheer and high along most of this 6-mile (10-km) stretch of the north Cornwall coast-line – up to 250 feet (76 m) in places, and topped by an area of flat heathland adjacent to the coast road. Colonies of sea-birds line the sheer cliff, and are particularly concentrated at Navax Point, Hell's Mouth and Ralph's Cupboard, Crag-nesting land-birds also breed on the cliff, and in some place land-slips have created an undercliff where other species of small land-bird can be seen.

Highlights
Close views of nesting **kittiwake** and auks at Hell's Mouth.

Time and season
Visit during the breeding season if possible. All year: **gannet, cormorant, herring gull, raven, meadow pipit, kestrel, oystercatcher.** Spring and summer: **fulmar, gannet, cormorant, shag, great black-backed gull, kittiwake, razorbill, guillemot, jackdaw, wren, rock pipit, wheatear.**

5 Pentire Head and Portquin Bay

LOCATION **About a mile (1.5 km) north of Polzeath, 12 miles (19 km) north-west of Bodmin.** *Landranger Sheet 200, 930810.*

Sea-birds breed in substantial numbers on the north-facing cliffs of this section of the Cornwall coast, where they are joined by crag-nesting land-birds – notably house martins – and by roosting birds of prey. The most interesting area is Rumps Point, a rocky headland crowned with an Iron Age fort. On the cliffs below the fort there is a small auk colony, and **puffins,** which nest on nearby islands, can be seen offshore.

In winter the area is also important for waders, and for corn bunting on the fields above the cliffs.

Highlights
Breeding auks and **gulls.**

Time and season
Visit during spring, when the colonies are at their noisiest. All year: **cormorant, oystercatcher, raven, meadow pipit.** Autumn and winter: birds of prey, **turnstone.** Spring and summer: **shag, kestrel, razorbill, guillemot, puffin, kittiwake.**

6 Willapark, Tintagel

LOCATION **About half-a-mile north of the town of Tintagel on Cornwall's northern coast.** *Landranger Sheet 200, 063898.*

Willapark has been described as 'a noble headland', and the description could not be more fitting: the rock rises some 300 feet (91 m) out of the sea, and overlooks the site of the most important auk colony in the South West. The nests are on Lye Rock, which is cut off from the mainland by a narrow channel, thus protecting the birds. Other sea-birds nest both here and on precipitous cliffs further along this beautiful and dramatic stretch of coast.

Highlights
Puffins nesting in their burrows.

Time and season
Visit during the breeding season. All year: **fulmar, cormorant, shag, kestrel, great black-backed gull, herring gull, raven, jackdaw.** Spring and summer: **razorbill, puffin, guillemot, lesser black-backed gull.**

7 Crackington Haven

LOCATION **On Cornwall's northern coast about 7 miles (11 km) south-west of Bude.** *Landranger Sheet 190, 142968.*

This is the wildest and most striking part of the north Cornwall coast-line: here High Cliff rises to over 700 feet (213 m). Crackington Haven itself is a sheltered inlet with a sandy beach exposed at low tide. The cliffs do not have many ledges, so there are few sea-birds nesting. However, **kestrels** nest here, and from the cliff tops there are good views towards Lundy Island where auks and **gulls** breed, so these birds may occasionally be seen offshore. Along the cliff top there is heathland, with areas of scrub and grass where you can in addition find an interesting variety of the smaller land-birds.

Highlights
Sea-birds soaring on the up-draft at the cliff edge south from Crackington Haven.

Time and season

In spring and autumn there is a chance to see a greater variety of migrants passing offshore. All year: **gannet, kestrel, lesser black-backed gull, herring gull, raven, jackdaw, wren, meadow pipit.**

DEVON

8 Hentor, Willings Wall and Trowlesworthy Warrens

LOCATION **The south-west flank of Dartmoor, about 10 miles (16 km) north-east of Plymouth.** *Landranger Sheet 202, 600655 and Outdoor Leisure Map: Dartmoor.*

On this large upland area, grass and grassy heathland dominate, with areas of bog and tors. Compared to other parts of Dartmoor, the area is not rich in wildlife habitats, but a characteristically upland bird community can be found after a climb. Hentor rises to 1,600 ft (488 m), and there are other similar exposed crags elsewhere in the area where birds of prey and **ravens** can be seen, particularly in summer. Take care when out walking – the site is very exposed and parts of it are some distance from roads.

Highlights

Kestrels and **buzzards** hovering in search of prey.

Time and season

Best during summer, when migrant species add variety and numbers to the year-round residents. All year: **kestrel, red grouse, raven, carrion crow, dipper.** Spring and summer: **buzzard, curlew, meadow pipit, wheatear, twite.**

DORSET

9 Portland Bill

LOCATION **Six miles (10 km) south of Weymouth.** *Landranger Sheet 194, 677686.*

Portland Bill is a rocky peninsula connected to the main coast-line by a narrow strip of land. The spot is therefore easily accessible, yet provides close looks at species of sea-birds in numbers usually seen only from a boat or an offshore island. Migrating birds – a few of them quite rare – can be seen in flight, or resting briefly. There is a staffed Bird Observatory in the old lighthouse, and birds are ringed and recorded here. Don't spend the whole visit looking out to sea – look inland too, and you may spot a very unusual migrant such as the sub-alpine warbler or the ortolan bunting.

Highlights

Massed seabirds and migrating rarities; **gannets** diving to feed; **puffins** flying to their nests in spring.

Time and season

Best August-October and March-May, though always good. All year: **puffin, razorbill, kestrel, gulls.** Winter: **purple sandpiper, red-throated diver,** wildfowl, **Slavonian grebe.** Spring: **common scoter, shag, pied flycatcher.** Autumn: **Manx shearwater, terns, gannet, skuas.**

10 Brownsea Island

LOCATION **The largest of several islands in Poole Harbour; reached by passenger ferry (fee) from Sandbanks.** *Landranger Sheet 195, 025880.* ADMISSION: **£0.80 landing charge.**

Poole Harbour provides shelter and safety for many thousands of wildfowl and waders, and Brownsea's central position makes it a popular roosting and nesting place, particularly for migrating birds. About 50 species of bird breed here, and a staggering total of 180 species have been seen on the island in recent years. The island is small – a little over a mile (1.5 km) long – and is virtually surrounded by sand and mudflats where many of the birds feed. There is unrestricted access to over half of the island, but the northern/north-eastern area is a Nature Reserve administered by the Dorset Naturalists' Trust, and access is restricted to tours guided by the warden. This area includes a ternery, reed beds, a salt-marsh and a lagoon. Rarities that have been observed on the island include the Dartford warbler and avocet.

Highlights

Rarities, ground-nesting **shelduck** and **herring gull** and very large flocks of wildfowl and waders.

Time and season

Winter for waders and wildfowl, high tide during autumn and spring for concentrations of migrants in the harbour. All year: **red-throated diver, Slavonian grebe, cormorant, shag, shelduck, wigeon, scaup, red-breasted merganser, redshank, black-headed gull, common gull, great black-backed gull, herring gull, lesser black-backed gull.** Winter: **eider, common scoter, ringed plover, grey plover, turnstone, sanderling, dunlin, bar-tailed godwit, curlew.** Spring: **greenshank.** Summer: **oystercatcher, common sandpiper, Sandwich tern, common tern, little tern, Arctic tern.** Autumn: **greenshank.**

SOMERSET

---

11 Holnicote Estate

LOCATION **Extending south-west for some 6 miles (10 km) from the north coast of Somerset, 3 miles (5 km) west of Minehead.** *Landranger Sheet 181, 900450.*

On this large coastal and moorland estate it is possible to observe a greater range of upland bird species than practically anywhere else in the South West. There is a remarkable diversity of rich wildlife habitats: the moorland is covered by vigorous heather, bilberry and gorse, and is dissected by ancient oak woodlands in the valleys. A cliff and shingle coast forms the northern border.

For upland birds, visit the south-west corner around Wilmersham Common and Dunkery Beacon, the highest point on Exmoor. The coastal birdlife is less exciting, but there is an extensive area of moorland behind the shore, so in a single visit to the coastal area around Selworthy Beacon and Hurlstone Point, it should be possible to see a range of both coastal and upland species. There is a chance too of spotting a few rarities – hobbys have been seen here recently.

Highlights

Red grouse – rare in the South West – and good moorland bird community.

Time and season

Spring and summer best for the upland species. All year: **fulmar, cormorant, buzzard, kestrel, red grouse, black grouse, black-headed gull, great black-backed gull, herring gull, stock dove, rock pipit, raven, carrion crow, jackdaw, dipper.** Winter: **shelduck, hen harrier, dotterel, golden plover, black redstart, fieldfare, snow bunting.** Spring and autumn: **dotterel, common sandpiper, dunlin, greenshank, pied flycatcher, wheatear, snow bunting.** Summer: **curlew.**

AVON

---

12 Middle Hope and Sand Point

LOCATION **On the south side of the Bristol Channel, about 2 miles (3 km) north of Weston-super-Mare.** *Landranger Sheet 182, 325660.* **Access from National Trust car park at the northern end of Sand Bay.**

Jutting out into the Bristol Channel, the low rock platform of Sand Point attracts numerous migrant birds in autumn and spring. To the east of the promontory, looking across towards Cardiff, there is a strip of mud which attracts many waders; and to the south, Sand Bay provides food and protection for wildfowl. Areas of scrub just inland conceal the nests of many smaller birds, and over twenty species – mostly tits, thrushes, finches and warblers – are known to breed here. The scrub area also functions as a secure resting place for birds in passage.

Highlights

Thousands of waders riding out storms in Sand Bay.

Time and season

Spring and autumn best for migrants; avoid holiday weekends, since the area is popular with picnickers. All year: **cormorant, shelduck, kestrel, oystercatcher,** lapwing, **curlew, great** and **lesser black-backed gulls, herring gull, jackdaw, wren,** meadow pipit, rock pipit. Spring and autumn: **Manx shearwater, storm petrel, gannet, golden plover, bar-tailed godwit, knot, sanderling, great skua, Arctic skua, black-headed gull, kittiwake, terns – common, Arctic, little** and **Sandwich, ring ouzel, wheatear.** Winter: **wigeon, eider, Brent goose, mute swan, grey plover, redshank, knot, dunlin, short-eared owl** and **snow bunting.**

THE SOUTH EAST

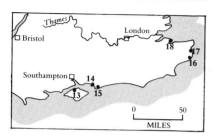

ISLE OF WIGHT

---

13 Newtown Estuary

LOCATION On the north-west coast of the Isle of Wight, about 5 miles (8 km) from Newport. *Landranger Sheet 196, 424906 and New Forest Outdoor Leisure map.*

Newtown Harbour, one of the most beautiful and unspoiled of the southern estuaries, includes an intricate system of tidal creeks, amounting to some 14 miles (23 km) in length. Extensive mud-flats are exposed at low water, and the estuary is fringed with salt-marsh, shingle, meadowland and oak woodland. The main appeal of the site is the large concentration of birds that winters in the shelter of the unpolluted estuary: peak numbers of wildfowl and waders have been known to reach 5,000 or more. **Gulls** roost here in large numbers, too. Part of the property is a Local Nature Reserve.

Highlights
Thousands of **dunlin** and lapwing, wintering dark-bellied **Brent geese**.

Time and season
Best between December and February, but also good for waders throughout spring and autumn. High tide concentrates birds near the shore. All year: **kestrel, herring gull, common gull, black-headed gull, jackdaw, carrion crow, stock dove, wren.** All seasons except summer: **oystercatcher, ringed plover, turnstone, redshank, greenshank, knot.** Winter: **black-throated diver, Slavonian grebe, cormorant, red-breasted merganser, shelduck, Brent goose, mute swan, grey plover, golden plover, curlew, bar-tailed godwit, dunlin, sanderling, kittiwake, razorbill, guillemot, short-eared owl, fieldfare.** Spring and autumn: **wheatear, common, Arctic** and **little terns,** rarities.

WEST SUSSEX

---

14 East Head

LOCATION On the eastern side of Chichester Harbour, close to the village of West Wittering. *Landranger Sheet 197, 766990.*

East Head is a low, sand-dune-covered promontory jutting out near the harbour entrance, and is on one of the few remaining unspoiled stretches of coast-line in West Sussex. It is surrounded by mud-flats and saltings, and looks westwards towards Hayling Island, where up to 10,000 waders and waterfowl roost. The bird population in the harbour swells dramatically with the arrival of migrants in spring and autumn, and with luck it is possible at these times to see some rarities. In winter, many waterfowl can be seen not far off shore.

Highlights
Up to 500 dark-bellied **Brent geese** in winter, migrants in autumn.

Time and season
As with any estuary, waders closest to the shore soon after high tide. Good at most times of year, but peak numbers in September, and large variety in winter. All year: **cormorant, shag, oystercatcher, dunlin, bar-tailed godwit.** Winter: **Brent goose, shelduck, wigeon, eider, red-breasted merganser, grey plover, turnstone, knot, sanderling, little stint.** Autumn: **ringed, golden** and **grey plovers, turnstone, knot, sanderling, little stint, greenshank, redshank, curlew.**

---

15 Pagham Harbour

LOCATION Pagham is a village on the outskirts of Bognor Regis. The harbour is immediately west of the town. *Landranger Sheet 197, 880976 and Outdoor Leisure Map: Purbeck.*

Pagham Harbour is a great place to take a novice bird-watcher – here it is possible to see in one day a greater range of species than almost anywhere else in the south. The wide variety of birds reflects the diversity of the habitats in the harbour and the surrounding areas: mud-flats and saltings support many species of coastal and wetland birds, but there are also large areas of pasture, scrub and reeds nearby, where finches, thrushes and birds of prey can be seen. Either walk along the path around the harbour, or view from the headland at Pagham or nearby Sidlesham Ferry.

Highlights

In autumn the number of species present is further swelled by migrant geese, sea-ducks and waders. **Short-eared owl** hunt over the fields.

Time and season

High tide brings waders closer to the shore; in winter visit morning or evening to see **Brent geese** on the mud-flats. All year: **shelduck, stock dove, kestrel.** Winter: **Brent goose, eider, hen harrier,** smew, **Slavonian grebe, red-breasted merganser, common scoter, grey plover, golden plover, turnstone, dunlin, bar-tailed god-wit, sanderling.** Spring: **turnstone, ringed plover.** Summer: **little tern, common tern, Sandwich tern.** Autumn: **little stint, greenshank, knot, short-eared owl.**

KENT

---

16 Bockhill Farm

LOCATION North of St Margaret's at Cliffe, mid-way between Dover and Deal. *Landranger Sheet 179, 370455.*

The main attraction of Bockhill Farm is the cliff-top walk from the Lighthouse and Coastguard Station. The path passes directly above the nests of many sea-birds, and though the nests themselves are not visible from the path, there are excellent views of the birds flying along the cliffs at eye level on their way to and from the nests.

Highlights

Close views of sea-birds in flight.

Time and season

Best in spring and summer. All year: **fulmar, herring gull, common gull, meadow pipit.** Summer: **lesser black-backed gull.**

---

17 Sandwich Bay

LOCATION Two miles (3 km) north-east of Sandwich; access via Princes Golf Club (toll road) or from New Downs Farm. *Landranger Sheet 179, 347620.*

On the low coastal land between Sandwich and Ramsgate, the winding River Stour has created a haven for waders: in addition to estuary mud and coastal grassland, there are areas of sand dunes, pebbly beaches, and both freshwater- and salt-marsh. **Terns** and several species of waders nest here, there is the usual complement of gulls, and in nearby Pegwell Bay it is possible to see **divers.** Part of the area is a Reserve administered by the Kent Trust for Nature Conservation.

In addition to coastal birds, Sandwich Bay is a landfall for migrating chats, thrushes, warblers and finches from the continent of Europe.

Highlights

Nationally-important wintering popula-tion of waders.

Time and season

The turn of the tide for waders; autumn for passing rarities. Winter: **red-throated diver, Brent goose, hen harrier, golden plover, grey plover, knot, sanderling, dunlin, redshank, bar-tailed godwit, curlew, snow bunting.** Spring: **oystercatcher, ring-ed plover, redshank, little tern.** Autumn: **little stint, greenshank.**

---

18 Shell Ness

LOCATION Shell Ness is about 2 miles (3 km) south-east of Leysdown on Sea, on the Isle of Sheppey in the Thames Estuary. *Landranger Sheet 178, 050670.*

The Isle of Sheppey is one of the most rewarding spots for bird-watching in the south; Shell Ness is at the extreme eastern end of the island. The sea wall provides a grandstand view of two distinct habitats: the seaward side looks out over large expanses of mud which are the winter home for numerous species of wader; inland, rough pasture is criss-crossed by dykes and drainage ditches, forming an invaluable refuge for passage migrants in autumn and spring, and for breeding pairs of waterfowl and waders.

Highlights

Massed waders, particularly in winter; spectacular flights of thousands of **knot;** courtship displays by **shelduck,** occasional rare migrants, huge movements of sea-birds in autumn.

Time and season

High tide brings waders closer inshore, dusk/dawn for **owls**. All year: **kestrel, oystercatcher, kittiwake, redshank.** Winter: **bar-tailed godwit, knot, grey plover, turnstone, Brent goose, wigeon, red-breasted merganser, eider, common scoter, hen harrier, short-eared owl, red-throated diver.** Spring: **bar-tailed godwit, turnstone.** Autumn: **little stint, grey plover, bar-tailed godwit, turnstone, gannet, Arctic skua.**

WALES

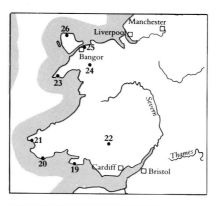

WEST GLAMORGAN

19 Worm's Head to Port-Eynon

LOCATION **Worm's Head is the extreme western tip of the Gower Peninsula, a mile or so (1.5 km) west of the village of Rhossili.** *Landranger Sheet 159, 383878.* **Port-Eynon Point is four-and-a-half miles (7 km) south-east at 468845.**

For three-and-a-half hours either side of low water, you can walk along a causeway on to the rocky promontory of Worm's Head to see the large cliff-face colony of auks and **gulls.** The rising tide, though, cuts this mile-long National Nature Reserve off from the headland, so check tide-tables before crossing. Even when Worm's Head is inaccessible, there is still plenty of birdlife to be seen from the low cliffs and raised beaches leading south-east to Port Eynon; in spring and autumn there are

terns, skuas and **shearwaters** offshore.

Highlights

Courting displays by **razorbills.**

Time and season

Low tide for crossing to Worm's Head. Activity reaches a peak in spring and summer. All year: **cormorant, shag, oystercatcher, turnstone, great black-backed gull, herring gull, lesser black-backed gull, black-headed gull, stock dove, carrion crow, jackdaw, meadow pipit.** Winter: **common scoter, curlew, purple sandpiper, fieldfare.** Spring: **Sandwich tern.** Spring and summer: **Manx shearwater, fulmar, kittiwake, guillemot, razorbill, puffin.** Autumn: **Manx shearwater, Sandwich tern, Arctic skua.**

DYFED

20 Stackpole

LOCATION **On the extreme southern edge of the Pembroke peninsula, about 6 miles (10 km) south of Pembroke.** *Landranger Sheet 158, 977963.*

This part of the Pembrokeshire coastline features a dramatic alternation between limestone cliffs and sandy, dune-fringed beaches. The main attraction is the cliff-nesting birds on the narrow ledges high above the sea in Stackpole National Nature Reserve. Members of the **crow** family can also be observed here. Away from the sea there are lakes, woods, grassland and farmland, supporting various warblers, buntings, finches and wildfowl. Much of the coast and inland area is a Nature Reserve, and open to the public.

Highlights
Colony of nesting auks and **gulls, choughs.**

Time and season
At low tide observation from beaches is easier – at high tide stay on the cliff-top. Birds most numerous in spring. All year: **fulmar, cormorant, shag, buzzard, kestrel, oystercatcher, great black-backed gull, herring gull, stock dove, rock pipit, chough, jackdaw, carrion crow, raven.** Winter: **shelduck, redshank.** Summer: **fulmar, razorbill, puffin, shag, lesser black-backed gull, kittiwake, guillemot.**

21 St David's Peninsula

LOCATION **Stretches of Dyfed's coast-line west and south of St David's including the northern side of St Bride's Bay.** *Landranger Sheet 157, 721278 to 840230.*

The sea-birds that nest along the narrow ledges of this rocky section of Dyfed's coast are not concentrated in noisy colonies: instead the breeding sites are scattered thinly at intervals along the cliffs. The best area to see nesting birds is on the south coast overlooking St Bride's Bay. Don't expect any surprises – there are no rare sea-birds here, though

you may see a pair of **chough.** For sea-watching, visit St David's Head to the north: besides birds flying offshore, you may spot grey seals, which breed to the north.

Highlights
Gulls returning to the nest, beaks brimming with food; land-birds nesting on the cliffs.

Time and season
Most rewarding in the spring and summer. All year: **fulmar, gannet, cormorant, buzzard, kestrel, great black-backed gull, herring gull, stock dove, raven, carrion crow, jackdaw, chough, rock pipit, wren.** Winter: **oystercatcher, snow bunting.** Spring and autumn: **common tern, ring ouzel.** Spring and summer: **lesser black-backed gull, meadow pipit, Lapland bunting.**

POWYS

22 Brecon Beacons

LOCATION **Eight thousand acres of crags and valleys east of the A470, Merthyr Tydfil to Brecon road.** *Landranger Sheet 141 – centred on Penyfan 013216; Outdoor Leisure Map: Brecon Beacons Central.*

The Brecon Beacons National Park is well known for its spectacular scenery, and this area of it is no exception. Birds of prey are ideally adapted to this environment, and here

their natural diet of small mammals and birds is boosted by the numerous dead sheep that litter the hillsides. Crags and screes may be the most striking aspect of the scenery, but do not overlook other bird habitats: most of the area is covered in grass or peat bog, and the valleys are wooded. Note: the area can be very dangerous, so take special care, particularly on the crags.

Highlights
Soaring birds of prey.

Time and season
Some species breed here, so visit in early summer. All year: **buzzard, kestrel, red grouse, raven, carrion crow, jackdaw, wren, dipper.** Spring and summer: **ring ouzel, wheatear, pied flycatcher, meadow pipit.**

GWYNEDD

23 Lleyn Peninsula

LOCATION **About 2 miles (3 km) west of the B4413 at Aberdaron.** *Landranger Sheet 123, 150280.*

Reached only by B-roads, this part of West Wales is fairly remote, so the birds that nest on the sea cliffs at the north side of the peninsula do so relatively undisturbed. The most interesting and varied colonies are roughly adjacent to the road between Capel Carmel and Pwlldefaid, where some land-birds share the rocks with the **gulls** and other sea-birds.

Highlights

Flocks of **chough** feeding on the grassy cliff-tops.

Time and season

Good most seasons, though numbers are probably highest in the summer. In spring and autumn migrants may broaden the range of species. All year: **fulmar, cormorant, shag, buzzard, kestrel, great black-backed gull, herring gull, raven, carrion crow, wren, chough, rock pipit.** Spring and summer: **kittiwake, razorbill, guillemot, Manx shearwater, lesser black-backed gull, wheatear, meadow pipit.**

24 The Migneint

LOCATION **About three-and-a-half miles (7 km) north-east of Ffestiniog, straddling the B4407 and B4406. *Landranger Sheets 115 and 116, 762439.***

This is part of the 25,000 acre Ysbyty Estate, a beautiful and remote area of moorland embracing upland heath, peat bog and grassy moor habitats between 1,000 and 1,600 ft (300-500 m). The undulating upper slopes are important breeding areas for upland birds, and part is designated a Site of Special Scientific Interest (SSSI)

Highlights

Good moorland bird community, **red grouse,** nesting waders, birds of prey.

Time and season

Visit during the spring and early summer when the birds are breeding, but take care not to disturb birds nesting on the ground. All year: **buzzard, kestrel, red grouse, black grouse.** All year bar winter: **golden plover, dunlin, curlew, common sandpiper, black-headed gull, wheatear.** Spring: **wheatear, ring ouzel.**

25 Carneddau

LOCATION **Eight miles (13 km) south-east of Bangor, between the A5 and A55. *Landranger Sheet 115, 670650.***

This vast tract of Snowdonia includes some of the finest scenery in Britain, but the barrenness and remoteness of the place protect the upland birds that live here. Several of the mountains within the area rise to over 3,000 ft (914 m) and most of the region is covered in upland grass, peppered with cliffs and outcrops of rock. For visitors, the remoteness is a hazard – take the usual precautions to ensure your own safety.

Highlights

Birds of prey, nesting **chough.**

Time and season

Birds most abundant and visible in summer, but more variety in winter. All year: **buzzard, kestrel, red grouse, raven, chough, meadow pipit.** Winter: **raven, carrion crow, fieldfare, snow bunting.** Spring: **curlew, common sandpiper, ring ouzel, wheatear, pied flycatcher.** Summer: **black-headed gull, common gull, jackdaw, twite.** Autumn: **golden plover, dotterel.**

26 Cemlyn

LOCATION **On the north coast of Anglesey, 2 miles (3 km) west of Cemaes Bay. *Landranger Sheet 114, 333933.***

The most striking feature of Cemlyn Bay is a half-mile long shingle bar which separates a brackish lagoon and salt-marsh from the sea. Terns breed here and the North Wales Naturalists' Trust administers the bay as a Nature Reserve. Wildfowl winter in the area, feeding on the adjacent low-lying rushy farmland which periodically floods. There is a winter Nature Trail starting at Bryn Aber specifically routed to give good views of the wildfowl.

Highlights

In summer, **terns** fishing offshore, hovering over the waves then plunge diving. In winter, the sheer variety of water birds.

Time and season

Most rewarding in winter and summer, though a good variety of migrants can be seen during the other seasons. All year: **red-breasted merganser, shelduck, mute swan, oystercatcher, ringed plover, grey plover, turnstone, curlew, redshank, herring gull, black-headed gull, meadow pipit.** Winter: **wigeon, long-tailed duck, golden plover, common gull, fieldfare.** Summer: **common, Arctic and Sandwich terns.**

MIDDLE ENGLAND

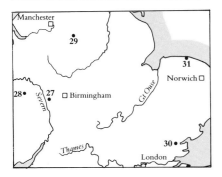

HEREFORD & WORCESTER

27 Clent Hills

LOCATION **South-west of Birming-ham, enclosed by the A456, M5 and A491.** *Landranger Sheet 139, 930790.*

This is a popular Country Park, with grassy hills, gorse, bracken and woodland. The large and varied bird community is dominated by lowland and woodland species, but several upland species can be seen passing through.

Highlights
Large variety of breeding birds.

Time and season
Visit early on spring mornings to see maximum activity. All year: **buzzard, kestrel, stock dove, carrion crow,** rook, **jackdaw, wren, meadow pipit.** Winter: **curlew, fieldfare.** Spring and autumn: **hen harrier, curlew, raven, fieldfare, wheatear, pied flycatcher.**

SHROPSHIRE

28 Long Mynd

LOCATION **Immediately east of Church Stretton, some 13 miles (22 km) south of Shrewsbury.** *Landranger Sheet 137, 410940.*

This windy, exposed upland moor rises to 1,700 ft (518 m) and is a good place to see birds of prey at close quarters, in addition to other common upland species. Little climbing is needed: roads go right over the top, but those who make the effort to walk up through the farmland and tree-lined valleys will also see a variety of woodland and grassland species.

Highlights
Buzzards searching for prey.

Time and season
All year: **buzzard, kestrel, red grouse, stock dove, meadow pipit, jackdaw, carrion crow, raven.** Winter: **fieldfare, short-eared owl.** Spring: **golden plover, curlew.** Summer: **dipper, pied flycatcher, wheatear, ring ouzel.**

DERBYSHIRE

29 Longshaw

LOCATION **About 2 miles (3 km) south-east of Hathersage, near** Grindleford BR station. *Landranger Sheets 110 and 119, 240800.*

Bordering on Hathersage Moor, the Longshaw Estate includes numerous areas of moorland, sloping grassland, low shrubs and bracken which provide protection and food for nesting upland birds and summer visitors. Additionally, nearby Burbage Rocks and Stanage Edge are suitable habitats for crag-nesting birds. **Owls** hunt over the area, and woodland on the lower slopes further increases the diversity of bird species to be seen here.

Highlights
Substantial population of breeding birds including **pied flycatchers.**

Time and season
Best spring/summer. All year: **kestrel, red grouse, stock dove, short-eared owl, carrion crow, jackdaw, wren, dipper.** Spring and summer: **curlew, common sandpiper, fieldfare, ring ouzel, wheatear, meadow pipit, pied flycatcher.**

ESSEX

30 Northey Island and the Blackwater Estuary

LOCATION **About one-and-a-half miles (2 km) east of Maldon. The island is reached by a causeway, and is cut off at high tide.** *Landranger Sheet 168, 872058.*

The Blackwater Estuary is an internationally important wintering ground for many thousands of waders and wildfowl. Northey Island itself is a Nature Reserve, and accessible only by prior appointment with the warden, but many species of birds can be seen from the mainland north or south of the estuary. The whole area is a maze of creeks and ditches, salt-marsh and mud-flats, so there is ample protection and cover for the many species of birds that roost here. In spring and autumn the species count is further boosted by migrants.

Highlights

Huge flocks of **Brent geese** and **shelduck**.

Time and season

Visit at high tide in winter to see the waders flying to roost, or during spring or autumn to spot migrants. Winter: **Slavonian grebe, Brent goose, shelduck, wigeon, red-breasted merganser, ringed plover, grey plover, turnstone, dunlin, redshank, curlew.** Spring: **red-throated diver, ringed plover, grey plover, golden plover, turnstone, dunlin, curlew.** Summer: **common tern.** Autumn: **ringed plover, grey plover, golden plover, turnstone, greenshank, redshank, curlew.**

NORFOLK

---

31 Blakeney and Morston

LOCATION **The Morston salt-marshes stretch for several miles adjacent to the A149, north Norfolk coast road. Blakeney Point is reached either by boat from Morston or from Blakeney, or else by walking the three-and-a-half miles (5.5 km) along the spit from Cley next the Sea.** *Landranger Sheet 133, 000460.*

This stretch of the north Norfolk coast is particularly rich in birdlife. Blakeney Point itself is a long sand spit which reaches out into the North Sea, sheltering dunes and salt-marsh on the mainland side. The spit is a Bird Sanctuary maintained by the National Trust, and there are large breeding colonies of **terns**. Two hides provide fine views, and there is an information centre and tea room.

The salt-marshes and Blakeney Harbour are more readily accessible to the casual visitor than the Sanctuary itself, and offer views of numerous waders, and, during autumn, the chance of seeing some rare migrants.

Highlights

Large flocks of **Brent geese** in January and February; and you may be lucky enough to sight rarer **grebes** and **osprey** in autumn.

Time and season

Aim to arrive between tides for best views of waders feeding. All year: **redshank, Slavonian grebe, oyster-catcher.** Winter: **Brent goose, bar-tailed godwit, dunlin, knot, Lapland bunting, turnstone, twite, wigeon.** Summer: **common, Sandwich** and **little terns, shelduck, ringed plover.** Autumn: **osprey, bar-tailed godwit.**

NORTHERN ENGLAND

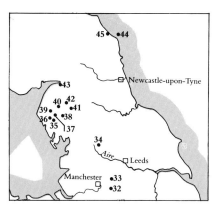

SOUTH YORKSHIRE

---

32 High Peak Estate

LOCATION **Astride the A57, midway between Sheffield and Manchester.** *Landranger Sheet 110, 100930* and *Outdoor Leisure Map: The Peak District, Dark Peak Area.*

This extensive area of peat and heather-covered upland adjacent to Kinder Scout is important as a breeding area for waders. The heather on the tops supports good numbers of grouse, and the parts of the moor that are managed for shooting are therefore sometimes closed to the public. Access is easiest from the south end of the Derwent Reservoir, or, avoiding a steep climb, from Snake Pass. Keep to footpaths.

Highlights

The variety of breeding waders.

Time and season
Best during spring and summer. Little of interest in winter. All year: **kestrel, red grouse, carrion crow, wren.** Spring and summer: **golden plover, curlew, common sandpiper, redshank, dunlin, black-headed gull, dipper, fieldfare, ring ouzel, wheatear, meadow pipit, twite.**

WEST YORKSHIRE

33 Marsden Moor

LOCATION **Seven miles (12 km) south-west of Huddersfield on the A62 and A640.** *Landranger Sheets 109 and 110, 020095.*

The Pennine Way passes through this large area of moorland on the northern fringes of the Peak District National Park. The scenery is typically Pennine in character, though there are few areas of bare rock. Upland birds to be seen in amongst the heather, or on the peat bog and in the air above it include **grouse**, waders and **pipits.** Birds of prey are rare.

The Pennine Way is clearly marked on Landranger maps.

Highlights
Grouse breeding on the moor.

Time and season
Visit during summer to see **grouse** and their young broods. All year: **red grouse.** Spring and summer: **dunlin, curlew, meadow pipit, ring ouzel.**

NORTH YORKSHIRE

34 Malham Tarn Estate

LOCATION **About two-and-a-half miles (4 km) north of Malham village, between Wharfedale and Ribblesdale.** *Landranger Sheet 98, 894673 and Outdoor Leisure Map: Malham and Upper Wharfedale.*

The Malham area is renowned for its outstanding natural beauty. A climb from any of the surrounding valleys takes the visitor on to a flat, dry limestone plateau, which supports a wide variety of upland birds. The tarn and adjacent marshland additionally attract a characteristic range of wetland birds. The Pennine Way passes through the estate, and there is a Field Centre at the edge of the Tarn, where the Field Studies Council runs a variety of residential bird-watching courses. Note: leave vehicles in valleys; car parking very limited on tops.

Highlights
The wide variety of birds that spend the summer in the area.

Time and season
Many more birds in summer than at other times, but avoid peak holiday periods. All year: **kestrel, red grouse, black-headed gull, common gull, jackdaw, carrion crow, wren.** All year except winter: **curlew, meadow pipit.** Summer: **golden plover, redshank, curlew, common sandpiper, dipper, wheatear, ring ouzel.**

CUMBRIA

35 Eskdale

LOCATION **The fells north of Boot in Eskdale, and Harter Fell south of Hardknott Pass.** *Landranger Sheet 89, 200030 and Outdoor Leisure Map: The English Lakes SW.*

The Eskdale fells combine most of the elements that are characteristic of the Lake District – small tarns surrounded by boggy peat; patches of heather; steep crags; rushing rivers and some gentle grassy slopes. The birds, too, are typical of the area; crag-nesting birds favour the northern parts above Great Moss, and a few waders are to be found breeding round the tarns; at Siney Tarn there is also a **black-headed gull** colony. Other 'specialists' inhabit their own favourite niches – **dippers** in the rivers, and **pied flycatchers** around the woodland areas. Be prepared for a few oddities, too: **red-throated diver, black-necked grebe, osprey** and goshawk have all been seen here.

Highlights
The **raven's** tumbling acrobatic courtship display.

Time and season
As with any upland area, you are likely to see more in spring and summer than at other times of the year. All year: **buzzard, red grouse, black grouse, raven, carrion crow, jackdaw, wren, dipper.** Winter: **fieldfare.** Spring and summer: **curlew, common**

sandpiper, black-headed gull, wheatear, pied flycatcher, meadow pipit.

36 Wasdale

LOCATION **The shores of Wastwater, and the fells on all sides; accessible only from the west.** *Landranger Sheet 89, 160060 and Outdoor Leisure Map: The English Lakes SW.*

Wasdale is one of the least disturbed areas in the Lake District, largely because it is virtually surrounded by mountains, including Seatallan, Great Gable and Scafell Pike. This cordon of rock protects the Wasdale upland birdlife from interference. **Gulls** also make their nests here, and waders breed on Nether Wasdale Common.

Highlights
From the northern shores of Wastwater, views of birds of prey in flight over the screes.

Time and season
Birds more numerous (and more easily seen) in the summer. All year: **buzzard, kestrel, raven, dipper.** Summer: **oystercatcher, curlew, common sandpiper, black-headed gull, ring ouzel.**

37 Scafell Group

LOCATION **Between Borrowdale and Wastwater.** *Landranger Sheet 89,* *210060 and Outdoor Leisure Map: English Lakes SW.*

Scafell is England's highest peak, rising to over 2,500 ft (762 m), and this is reflected in the range of birds to be seen here. The craggy slopes, screes and boulder fields are only sparsely covered in vegetation and few birds breed in this inhospitable terrain: most of the bird population are either summer visitors, or else forage for food on the mountain before returning to nests in more hospitable areas of the Lake District.

Highlights
Nesting **ring ouzels,** chance to see other upland species in a true mountain habitat.

Time and season
Birdlife most profuse in summer; dangerous in winter for the inexperienced or ill-equipped. All year: **raven, wren.** Winter: **Lapland bunting.** Spring and summer: **ring ouzel.** Summer: **meadow pipit, wheatear.**

38 Lord Lonsdale's Commons

LOCATION **Either side of Grasmere, crossed by the A591 and B5343.** *Landranger Sheet 90.*

This vast National Trust property includes some of the most beautiful and rugged scenery in the Cumbrian Mountains. The whole area, from the summit of Bow Fell in the west to Dunmail in the east, is predominantly grass, and bracken heath, so many of the waders that are common in summer on lower, boggier fells cannot be seen here. Otherwise the region is well supplied with upland bird life, and there are no special spots for viewing particular species. Nevertheless, a walk which takes in a variety of different habitats, including crags, scree, mire, and valley areas is likely to yield the most varied sightings.

Highlights
Birds of prey, nesting **ravens.**

Time and season
Spring and summer are best, though **snow buntings** can sometimes be seen in winter. Avoid holiday periods if possible, since this area is very popular. All year: **buzzard, kestrel, red grouse, stock dove, raven, carrion crow.** Winter: **snow bunting.** Spring and summer: **ring ouzel, wheatear, black redstart, meadow pipit.**

39 Ennerdale

LOCATION **In the north-western Lake District above and to the east of Ennerdale Water.** *Landranger Sheet 89, 150140 and Outdoor Leisure Map: The English Lakes NW.*

This large area of National Trust land stretches like a collar around Ennerdale Water, and includes many summits and ridges reaching nearly 3,000 ft (over 900 m), boulder fields and some screes. There are many fast-flowing streams, a few small tarns and a lot of grassy open fell land and heather. There are a few areas of farmland and woodland, and at these spots you can expect to see some of the commoner lowland birds in addition to upland species.

Highlights
Ring ouzel singing in desolate boulder fields.

Time and season
More birdlife to be seen in the summer. All year: **kestrel, carrion crow, raven.** Winter: **snow bunting, fieldfare.** Summer: **ring ouzel, dipper, common sandpiper, wheatear, meadow pipit.**

40 Derwentwater and Borrowdale

LOCATION **Either side of the Derwentwater valley, about 4 miles (7 km) south and south-west of Keswick.** *Landranger Sheet 89,* **access to upland easiest from Honister Pass 225135; Watendlath 275162; Seathwaite 235122 and Stonethwaite 263137.**

Like much of the Lake District, the fells and valleys around Derwentwater encompass great contrasts of scenery and habitat within a small area, and there is a correspondingly broad range of birdlife. In the crags and fells you can see most of the commoner upland birds, but do not overlook woodland birds on the climb up, and water-birds on the tarns and lakes.

Highlights
Birds of prey, breeding waders.

Time and season
Interesting all year, but best in summer. All year: **hen harrier, buzzard, red grouse, short-eared owl, meadow pipit, carrion crow, raven, wren, dipper.** Winter: **fieldfare, snow bunting.** Spring: **oystercatcher, dotterel, golden plover, redshank, curlew, ring ouzel.** Summer: **oystercatcher, golden plover, redshank, curlew, wheatear, ring ouzel.** Autumn: **black-necked grebe, golden plover, curlew.**

41 Gowbarrow and Glencoyne

LOCATION **Adjacent to the western shores of Ullswater at the south end, and stretching up the fell as far as Stybarrow Dodd.** *Landranger Sheet 90, 400200 and Outdoor Leisure Map: The English Lakes NE.*

Stybarrow Dodd is a peak in the Helvellyn chain, and rises 2,000 ft (610 m) above the Ullswater valley. Between the lake shores and the mountain top lie wood, heath, grass, crag and stream habitats, so the range of birdlife is rich and varied. Some upland birds breed here, including **dipper** at the popular Aira Force waterfall, which drops 65 ft (20 m) close to the A5091. Sharp-eyed observers may be rewarded with a view of **golden eagles.**

Highlights
Birds in passage adding to the already long roll-call of species.

Time and season
Most interesting in the spring and early summer. All year: **red-breasted merganser, buzzard, kestrel, red grouse, curlew, stock dove, raven, carrion crow, jackdaw, wren, dipper, meadow pipit.** Winter: **cormorant, wigeon, great black-backed gull, lesser black-backed gull, herring gull, common gull, black-headed gull, fieldfare.** Spring and autumn: **mute swan, oystercatcher, golden plover, common sandpiper, redshank, gulls** (as winter), **wheatear, pied flycatcher.** Summer: **oystercatcher, common sandpiper, redshank, wheatear, pied flycatcher.**

42 Great Mell Fell

LOCATION **About 2 miles (3 km) south-west of Penruddock, close to the A66 from Penrith to Keswick.** *Landranger Sheet 90, 390250 and Outdoor Leisure Map: The English Lakes NE.*

This gently-sloping hill is topped by an area of peat bog, and is wooded at one side. Birdlife is abundant considering the altitude – the hill is over 1,450 ft (442 m) above sea-level – though there is not the diversity of species that can be seen on lower fells. In addition to upland birds, there are many woodland species, and you may see barn owls hunting over the hill.

Highlights
Birds of prey.

Time and season
Birdlife most abundant in summer, but

less inaccessible than some other high fells, so winter visits more practical. All year: **buzzard, kestrel, raven, carrion crow, wren.** Summer: **meadow pipit.**

43 Solway Commons

LOCATION **On the southern shore of the Solway Firth, about 12 miles (20 km) west of Carlisle.** *Landranger Sheet 85, 310560.*

One of Britain's greatest estuaries, the Solway Firth is of international importance for its large wintering population of wildfowl (especially geese) and waders. Although perhaps Caerlaverock National Nature Reserve is the best-known site on the Firth, the Solway Commons include an extensive stretch of the Cumbrian shore with one of the highest salt-marsh sections, Burgh Marshes, and the sand flats of Cardurnock Bay.

Highlights
Wintering **geese, ducks,** and waders on the flats, breeding waders on the marshes.

Time and season
March and April are the best months to see the **geese** on the south side of the Solway. Mud-flats very wide, so essential to view at high tide when waders are close to the shore. Autumn, winter and spring: **barnacle goose, shelduck, scaup, ringed plover, golden plover, knot, sanderling, bar-tailed godwit, redshank, greenshank, turnstone,** **wigeon.** Spring and summer: **shelduck, scaup, redshank,** lapwing, dunlin, oystercatcher, ringed plover, curlew, Arctic tern, meadow pipit.

NORTHUMBERLAND

44 Farne Islands

LOCATION **Two to 5 miles (3 to 8 km) off the coast of Northumberland. Boat departs from Seahouses, weather permitting (fee). Ring 0665 720424 for details.** *Landranger Sheet 75, 230370.*

There are 30 Farne Islands in all, and though some are hardly more than rocks, a few are big enough to land on, and have cliffs, beaches and a little grassland. Twenty-odd species of bird nest here, mainly auks, **gulls** and **terns,** but a few waders too. Some nest in large numbers, and most can be viewed at very close quarters. During the spring and autumn there are many migrants to be seen, including chats, and warblers. Two of the islands – Inner Farne Island and Staple Island – are open to the public from April to September, but with carefully-controlled arrangements between mid-May and mid-July.

Highlights
The **roseate tern,** one of Britain's rarer breeding birds.

Time and season
Best at the end of June or early July when the birds are feeding young. All year: **fulmar, cormorant, shag, eider, oystercatcher, ringed plover, herring gull, kittiwake, rock pipit.** Winter: **red-** and **black-throated divers, common scoter, turnstone, purple sandpiper.** Spring and autumn: **red-** and **black-throated divers, Manx shearwater, common scoter,** turnstone, whimbrel, **Arctic skua, great skua, gulls, terns.** Summer: **Sandwich, common, Arctic** and **roseate terns, lesser black-backed gull, guillemot, razorbill, puffin.**

45 Lindisfarne (Holy Island)

LOCATION **About 17 miles (27 km) south-east of Berwick-upon-Tweed, and linked to the A1 coast road by a causeway.** *Landranger Sheet 75, 136417.*

Lindisfarne is technically an island only when the tide rises; at other times all that separates Holy Island from the Northumberland coast is an expanse of mud and sand. For this reason the birds to be seen here are those which you might expect to find on an estuary, rather than on an offshore island in the true sense. Sheltered by Lindisfarne and flanking spits of land, Holy Island Sands is popular with waders, and in the winter there are vast flocks of wildfowl here. Few birds breed on the island, but many roost and feed there.

Highlights
Large numbers of light-bellied **Brent geese** in late winter.

Time and season

Without a boat, the island can be approached only at low tide. Most interesting in autumn and winter. Winter: **red-throated diver, Slavonian grebe, Brent goose, shelduck, mute swan, wigeon, eider, long-tailed duck, common scoter, red-breasted merganser.** Spring: **shelduck, scaup, oystercatcher, ringed plover, golden plover.** Autumn: **barnacle goose, shelduck, grey plover, knot, sanderling, little stint, dunlin, bar-tailed godwit.**

SCOTLAND

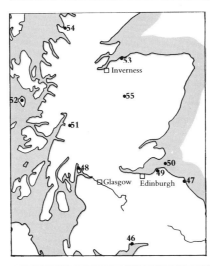

DUMFRIES & GALLOWAY

46 Caerlaverock

LOCATION On the north coast of the Solway, some 6 miles south of Dumfries on the B725. *Landranger Sheet 84, 052656.*

At Caerlaverock the River Nith and Lochar Water flow across a wide area of salt-marsh and mud, and into the Solway Firth. The marsh is famous for the enormous numbers of **geese** – sometimes over 10,000 – that over-winter there. The area is a Nature Reserve, and there is no free access to the mud-flats and marsh. This is partly for safety reasons – the mud-flats are dangerous. However, viewing facilities are excellent, and provide visitors with a very close look at the birds. The road from Dumfries runs alongside the Nith Estuary, and many birds can be seen without entering the sanctuary area.

Highlights

Ten thousand or more **barnacle geese** in winter; wildfowl species count often well into double figures.

Time and season

Best in autumn and winter. All year: **oystercatcher, golden plover, knot, curlew, redshank.** Winter: **peregrine falcon, merlin, hen harrier, barnacle goose, wigeon** and other wildfowl.

BORDERS

47 St Abb's Head

LOCATION St Abb's Head is about three-and-a-half miles (5.5 km) off the A1 between Berwick-on-Tweed and Dunbar. *Landranger Sheet 67, 913673.*

The 300-ft-high cliffs at St Abb's Head provide nesting sites for thousands of sea-birds, and just a short walk out of the village gives the visitor spectacular views of this important colony. The site is a Nature Reserve, and the best route around the cliffs is clearly marked. A loch on the top of the cliffs is home for a few waterfowl, for some duck in winter, and is used as a bathing- and resting-place for the large summer **kittiwake** population.

Highlights

Excellent views of nesting sea-birds at close quarters.

Time and season

Most of the breeding birds have departed by late July, so early summer is the best time to visit. All year: **shag.** Winter: **eider, oystercatcher, redshank, turnstone, purple sandpiper.** Spring: **wheatear, puffin, oystercatcher, redshank, turnstone, purple sandpiper, eider, gannet, Arctic skua, Manx shearwater, guillemot, kittiwake, razorbill.** Summer: **wheatear, guillemot, razorbill, puffin, kittiwake.** Autumn: **gannet, eider, skua, Manx shearwater, oystercatcher, redshank, turnstone, purple sandpiper.**

STRATHCLYDE

---

48 Argyll Forest Park

LOCATION **About 20 miles (30 km) north-west of Dumbarton, astride the A83, and enclosed by Loch Goil and Loch Long.** *Landranger Sheet 56, 270030.*

Despite the name, the majority of this Nature Reserve is open moorland and mountain: Forestry Commission planting is limited to the lower slopes. The Park is hemmed in by sea lochs, so there is some wildfowl interest in winter, and woodland birds including the **capercaillie** are to be found in forest areas. However, the upland species

are the stars, and are visible only after a strenuous climb: the 'Arochar Alps' rise to over 3,000 ft (over 900 m). On the upper slopes lucky visitors may see **ptarmigan,** which are present here in small numbers.

Highlights

Peregrine falcon dropping like a stone on to its prey.

Time and season

Open access all year, but few interesting passage birds, so summer or winter visits are probably best. All year: **hen harrier, buzzard, golden eagle, kestrel, peregrine falcon, red grouse, ptarmigan, black grouse, capercaillie, raven, carrion crow, short-eared owl.** Winter: **shelduck, wigeon, eider, red-breasted merganser.** Spring and summer: **oystercatcher, curlew, common sandpiper, meadow pipit, dipper, wheatear, ring ouzel, twite.**

LOTHIAN

---

49 Aberlady Bay

LOCATION **On the A198 from Edinburgh to North Berwick.** *Landranger Sheet 66, 465831.*

An indication of the importance of this tidal estuary can be gathered immediately from the baldest of statistics: 55 species of bird breed here, and a further 170 are either regular visitors or have been observed as passage

migrants. The variety is due not only to the location on the Firth of Forth, but also to the pattern of coastal deposition to be found here: behind the mud-flats there are saltings, and further inland, sand-dunes and mature grassland. The Reserve is open virtually all the year, through small parts are occasionally closed to the public. The best place for an overall view of the Bay is probably Gullane Point on the northern side.

Highlights

Thousands of **scoter** offshore in winter.

Time and season

Visit in autumn for the greatest variety, or in winter for wildfowl. Winter: **eider, shelduck, wigeon, common scoter, red-breasted merganser, knot, bar-tailed godwit.** Spring and summer: **eider, shelduck, ringed plover, dunlin, redshank, common, Arctic and little terns.** Autumn: **grey plover, knot, little stint, dunlin, Arctic and great skuas, terns, black-necked and Slavonian grebes.**

---

50 Bass Rock

LOCATION **In the Firth of Forth one-and-a-half miles (2.5 km) offshore.** *Landranger Sheet 67, 603872.* **Access by boat (fee) – see below for details.**

The lighthouse-keeper on Bass Rock is not short of company – he shares the quarter-square-mile island with 18,000 **gannets. Gulls** and auks also nest on the 250 ft- (76 m-) high cliffs around the island, though in smaller numbers. Visitors reach the island by boat and during the summer there are two or three trips a day, weather permitting. Call North Berwick (0620) 2838 for departure times.

Highlights
Rare opportunity to see nesting sea-birds at close quarters.

Time and season
Best in spring and summer. No winter boat service. Spring and summer: **fulmar, gannet, shag, kittiwake, razorbill, guillemot, puffin.**

HIGHLAND

---

51 Glen Coe

LOCATION **Running south-east and east from Loch Leven and the village of Glencoe.** *Landranger Sheet 41, 127565.*

The mountains that enclose Glen Coe are some of the most spectacular and imposing in Britain, rising to over 3,800 ft (1,158 m). T.S. Eliot wrote of the area 'Here the crow starves', but in fact the glen and surrounding moors manage to support not only numerous hooded crows, but a number of other upland birds besides. Birds of prey are most likely to be seen in flight, but on the ground you may see waders in summer, or snow-white **ptarmigan** in winter. Take special heed of the warnings on page 10 regarding precautions for upland walking, as the Glen can be very

dangerous, as witnessed by the mountain rescue team based here.

Highlights
Buzzards and **eagles** soaring above the higher crags.

Time and season
In summer birdlife is more abundant, and walking safer. All year: **buzzard, kestrel, ptarmigan, short-eared owl, raven, snow bunting.** Spring and summer: **dotterel, golden plover, curlew, meadow pipit, dipper, common sandpiper, wren, twite.**

---

52 Isle of Rhum

LOCATION **In the Inner Hebrides. Day-trips from Mallaig.** *Landranger Sheet 39, 370980.*

Rhum's isolation, and variety of soil and vegetation types makes it a favourite spot for scientific study, and there has been a Nature Reserve here for over 20 years. A permit is required to visit certain parts of the island, but a large area is open to the public. Rhum is large and mountainous – Askivall rises to 2,663 ft (812 m) – so it is possible to see not only coastal species, but many land-birds, too, and a full list of even just the breeding species would be too long to reproduce here.

Highlights
Enormous colony of **Manx shear-waters** – some estimates put the population as high as a quarter-of-a-million birds.

Time and season
Best in the summer. All year: **fulmar, shag, eider, golden eagle, peregrine falcon, merlin, red grouse, oyster-catcher, ringed** and **golden plovers, curlew, great black-backed gull, black guillemot, meadow** and **rock pipits, raven.** Spring and summer: **red-throated diver, Manx shear-water, shelduck, razorbill, guillemot, puffin, wheatear.**

---

53 Culbin Bar

LOCATION **About 8 miles (13 km) north-east of Inverness, in the Moray Firth.** *Landranger Sheet 27, 905575.*

These two shifting shingle bars run for nearly 5 miles (8 km) along the south side of the Moray Firth, and between the bars and the mainland there is an area of salt-marsh and sand-flats. Combined with the mild climate, these habitats would be sufficient in themselves to lure large numbers of birds to the area, but the diversity of species is further increased by the proximity of the Culbin Forest. This extends some distance inland from the coast and embraces two freshwater lochs. Sea-duck, **terns** and waders are the main attractions on the bar and saltings, but there are many land-birds, too.

DO NOT SMOKE IN THE FOREST

Highlights
Sandwich and **Arctic tern** in summer; whooper swans in winter.

Time and season

Good all year, though the seasonal variations may determine when you wish to visit. All year: **kestrel, buzzard, capercaillie, ringed plover, knot, dunlin, curlew, short-eared owl, crested tit.** Winter: **wigeon, long-tailed duck, oyster-catcher, bar-tailed godwit, little stint.** Spring/summer: **common scoter, redshank, Arctic, Sandwich, common, little terns.** Autumn: **common scoter, greenshank, little stint.**

54 Inverpolly

LOCATION **Stretching inland from the north-west coast about 10 miles (16 km) north of Ullapool.** *Land-ranger Sheet 13, 130120.*

This is one of Britain's wildest places, yet the range of birds to be seen is wide because the Reserve encompasses habitats ranging from crag and bog to seashore and island. In all, 104 bird species have been recorded here, and wild cats and pine martens patrol the peaks. Access to the main Reserve area is not easy, as the paths that there are get little use. However, much can be seen from the roads around the edges of the Reserve. In September and October public access is restricted – ring 057 14 204 or 085 484 234 for detailed information.

Highlights

Breeding sea- and upland birds.

Time and season

Summer visits advisable. All year:

golden eagle, buzzard, ptarmigan, raven. Winter: **barnacle geese.** Spring and summer: **black-throated diver, fulmar, shag, wigeon, red-breasted merganser, golden plover, greenshank, black guillemot, wheatear, ring ouzel.**

GRAMPIAN

---

55 Cairngorms

LOCATION **South-east of Aviemore.** *Landranger Sheet 36, 980090 and Outdoor Leisure Map: Aviemore and the Cairngorms.*

This Nature Reserve is vast – 10 miles square – and almost Arctic in character. Moorland predominates, but vegetation is very sparse on the peaks, which rise to over 4,000 ft (1,219 m). In addition to the usual upland species, careful observers will see **ptarmigan** and **dotterel** on the summits, and **black grouse** and **capercaillie** breed in the native pine forests to the north and north-east, and around Loch An Eilein. Above the tree-line birds of prey are common. Take special care about safety when walking – even in summer a change in the weather can make the moors very inhospitable, and though many parts of the Cairngorms are developed for skiing and tourism, other areas are quite remote.

Highlights

Ptarmigan moulting in autumn.

Time and season

Some areas closed to the public August to October for deer cull. Low cloud often restricts visibility, so clear summer weather most favourable. All year: **buzzard, ptarmigan, black grouse, red grouse, capercaillie, wren.** Winter: **snow bunting.** Summer: **dotterel, greenshank, ring ouzel, crested tit.**

ULSTER

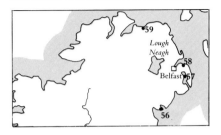

CO DOWN

56 Blockhouse Island and Green Island

LOCATION About 15 miles (24 km) south-east of Newry on the B27; J254097.

Because of the risk of disturbance, there is currently no public access to the RSPB Reserve but the numerous terns that nest here can be seen from neighbouring Greencastle Point. The two shingle islands are situated close to where Carlingford Lough meets the sea, so the usual species of sea-bird feed and roost in the area.

Highlights
Possibility of seeing the rare **roseate tern.**

Time and season
Ternery occupied only during spring and summer, but there is also an interesting population of overwintering species. All year: **black guillemot.** Winter: **red-throated diver, black-throated diver, scaup, common scoter.** Spring and summer: **ringed plover, Sandwich tern, roseate tern, common tern, Arctic tern.**

57 Strangford Lough

LOCATION Some 20 miles (32 km) south-east of Belfast; J560615.

To overstate the importance to bird-life of this large sea lough would be difficult. For example, it has been estimated that up to 40 per cent of the world's pale-bellied **Brent geese** may be seen feeding on the eel grass here at any one time, and there are nationally- and internationally-important populations of other wildfowl and waders. The Lough is connected to the sea at the southern end by a narrow channel, and has numerous small rocky islands and muddy inlets. The area is a Bird Sanctuary, and though public access to the shore is unlimited, visitors are asked to minimize disturbance by watching from the seven refuges.

Highlights
Overwintering waders and wildfowl, breeding **terns,** including the rare **roseate.**

Time and season
Never disappointing, but greatest numbers in autumn and winter. Autumn and winter: **mute swan, Brent goose, shelduck, wigeon, red-breasted merganser, ringed plover, golden plover, grey plover, knot, dunlin, redshank, greenshank, bar-tailed godwit, curlew.** Spring and summer: **corncrake, common tern, Arctic tern, roseate tern, Sandwich tern, black guillemot, rock pipit.**

58 Lighthouse Island

LOCATION Just outside the mouth of Belfast Lough. To visit (fee) contact the Boat Officer on Belfast 655081; J596858.

Almost all species of Northern Ireland birds have been recorded at the Observatory on Lighthouse Island, but for the visitor, the sea-birds are the main attraction. **Manx shearwaters** breed on the low cliffs in large numbers, as do many **gulls.** Inland, there are areas of grass and scrub that support a few nesting land-birds, including swallows and **wrens.**

The Observatory is staffed most weeks of the spring and autumn, when migration brings rarities on to the island, and in the summer there are frequent day trips for visitors.

Highlights
Shearwaters emerging from their burrows at dusk.

Time and season
Always good, but access easiest in the summer. All year: **oystercatcher, common gull, great black-backed gull, herring gull, black guillemot, stock dove, wren.** Winter: **shelduck, eider, red-breasted merganser.** Spring and summer: **fulmar, Manx shearwater, lesser black-backed gull, rock pipit.** Spring and autumn: **storm petrel, meadow pipit.**

CO LONDONDERRY

59 Bar Mouth

LOCATION On the north coast, 2 miles (3 km) east of Casterlock, at the mouth of the River Bann; C792355.

Mud-flats exposed at low tide in this small estuary provide rich pickings for waders, and a variety of species spend the winter here. Nearby grassland includes a broad mixture of plant types, thus attracting a diversity of the common smaller land-birds, and birds of prey. Migration sometimes brings rarer specimens here – visitors in the past have included green, curlew and wood sandpipers. There is a permanent hide from which the birds can be observed without risk of disturbance.

Highlights
Close views of waders feeding.

Time and season
Best during autumn and spring when birds in passage swell the numbers. All year: **herring gull,** birds of prey. Winter: **dunlin, redshank, bar-tailed godwit, curlew.** Spring and autumn: **sanderling,** rarities.

REPUBLIC OF IRELAND

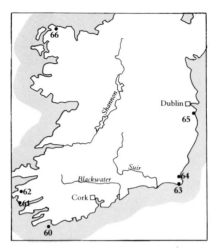

CO CORK

60 Cape Clear Observatory

Off the Cork coast – daily boat from Baltimore. Accommodation available. Enormous numbers of birds including albatross can be seen offshore during passage season.

CO KERRY

61 Little Skellig

Eighteen-thousand breeding pairs of **gannet, 1,000 kittiwake.** Boats (fee) leave from Portmagee. Landing on the island is not permitted.

62 Puffin Island

Eleven species of sea-birds breeding – **storm petrel, Manx shearwater, puffin,** and some land-birds including **raven** and **chough.** Boats leave from Portmagee.

CO WEXFORD

63 Wexford Slobs

North and south of Wexford Harbour. Salt-marsh and low-lying pasture that floods in winter. Migrants, waders in passage, large numbers of wildfowl, breeding **terns.**

64 South Wexford

Area of lakes and islands on the south coast. Auks, **Manx shearwater,** waders, sea-ducks, **terns** and **gulls.** Islands accessible by boat from Kilmore Quay.

CO DUBLIN

65 Dublin Bay area

Several interesting places from which to watch sea-birds, all within easy reach of Dublin itself.

Howarth Peninsula – **fulmar, guillemot, razorbill, black guillemot.**

Understanding birds

Dun Laoghaire Harbour – sea-ducks, **divers** and **purple sandpiper.**

To reach the following sites, take a boat (fee) from Howth Harbour or Rush.

Bull Island – pale-breasted **Brent geese** in winter,with other **ducks** and waders. **Snow** and **Lapland buntings.**

Ireland's Eye – **puffins.**

Lumbay – waders, **divers,** auks, **buntings** and sea-duck.

CO MAYO

66 Illanmaster

Puffin, barnacle geese. Landing on this island requires a permit from the Irish Wildlife Conservancy.

It is a bird's feathers that make it unique. There are other animals which fly, sing, make nests, lay eggs or migrate. But only birds have feathers. The nearest any other creature comes to having feathers is the reptile with its scales. Feathers probably evolved from scales, and birds and reptiles such as crocodiles and dinosaurs, for all their immense differences, shared a common ancestor.

Scientists are unable to tell exactly how the change from scales to feathers took place. Fossils of *Archaeopteryx,* the first known bird, shows that 150 million years ago feathers were already the same as they are today. But *Archaeopteryx* was no ordinary bird. Although it had feathers, it still had the teeth and long, bony tail of a reptile. Its breastbone was poorly developed and lacked the deep keel to which the flight muscles of modern birds are anchored. This suggests that at best it could only flap its wings weakly. Probably it relied mostly on gliding.

Their mastery of the air is the main reason why birds have been one of nature's most spectacular successes, evolving into thousands of different species and colonising every corner of the globe. In every aspect of their physiology, they reveal how perfectly they are adapted for flight. Some bones which were separate in their flightless ancestors – including bones in the wings and sections of the backbone – are now fused together, giving greater strength. Others are hollow and strutted, combining strength with lightness. Massive breast muscles power their wings, while their hearts keep pace with their intense energy, beating with fantastic rapidity; in the case of a robin's heart, for instance, more than eight times as fast as a man's. Birds' eyesight is also the most acute in the animal world, adapted to gathering information at the same high speed at which they live.

Speed, infinite mobility and wildness: these are the characteristics common to all birdlife, which make birds so fascinating to watch. Birds rarely remain still, except when they are roosting or incubating their eggs, and they are always on the alert. But their actions are never without meaning; every movement a bird makes has an exact purpose. One of the greatest satisfactions in bird-watching is understanding why birds behave as they do – learning to tell the difference between threat and courtship displays, for instance, or observing how they look after their feathers or build their nests.

Bird classification

It is now established that there are some 8,600 different kinds of birds in the world. At one time the number was put as high as 25,000, partly because the same bird had different names in different parts of the world. This was before the modern system of classification had been developed, which groups birds according to their evolutionary relationship with one another, and gives each of them a set of scientific names.

The basic unit of the modern system is the species, an interbreeding group of identical birds. The next, larger division is the genus, a group of closely related species of birds, usually showing obvious similarities. The black-headed gull, for instance, is one of many species belonging to the gull genus. A bird's scientific name always states the genus first, then the species. The black-headed gull is called *Larus ridibundus* – translated, the name means 'Gull, laughing'.

When one genus closely resembles another, they are grouped together to make a family. Gulls are similar in many ways to terns, and both belong to the family *Laridae,* named after the Greek word for a gull; in some schemes of classification they are separated into sub-families, *Larinae* (gulls) and *Sterninae* (terns). The families are grouped into 27 different orders. The family of gulls and terns belongs, together with a great variety of other sea- and shore-birds, in the order *Charadriiformes,* after the Greek for 'plover'. All the orders together make up the class *Aves* – 'Birds'.

Keeping records

To become a really proficient bird-watcher, it is important to keep a field notebook, such as this one, and to keep a logbook at home in which to write up your notes in greater detail. Your notebooks will soon become an invaluable fund of knowledge.

At the end of each year, check through your notes to see if they are worth sending to the records committee of your local bird-watching society. The annual bird reports of these societies, combined on a national level, often form the basis on which professional ornithologists establish the current status of a species.

Taking part in a census

Once you have become experienced at bird-watching you may wish to take part in a detailed census, organised at a local or national level. A census can take the form of a monthly count of birds at a reservoir or estuary, to check on the numbers of wildfowl or waders, for instance; or in the spring and summer months it may entail finding out the breeding population of a particular area. One such census is the Nest Record Scheme, co-ordinated by the British Trust for Ornithology, which aims to establish the exact breeding status of all British birds. If you wish to join this scheme, contact the BTO at Beech Grove, Tring, Hertfordshire.

Alternatively, you may prefer to start your own project. This could take the form of a census of the birds seen in your garden at different times of the year, or you could study the change in the type and number of birds on land undergoing development. Bird populations are always fluctuating, and keeping track of the changes taking place around you can be a fascinating pastime.

Bird ringing

The method of catching birds and ringing them – putting a light metal band on one leg – has been in use since the end of the 19th century, as a way of studying bird behaviour and migrations and to help in the conservation of particular species. Ringing birds has enabled conservationists to find out where certain species stop to rest while on migration; and international agreements between governments have made some of these stop-over points into nature reserves, to help to ensure the survival of the species.

The most common way of trapping birds in order to ring them is by using mist-nets – black nylon or terylene nets which are almost invisible to a bird in flight. The ringer quickly and carefully removes the trapped bird from the net, then fits the ring on its leg. The ring carried the address of the BTO, and a number which is unique to that bird. Before being released, the bird is identified and weighed and full details are taken of its age, sex and condition. The records are then sent for processing and storage to the BTO. If you wish to become a ringer yourself, you must be trained by a recognised expert and obtain a permit from the BTO. As co-ordinators of the ringing scheme the BTO will be able to supply any information which you may require.

If you ever find a dead, ringed bird, remove the ring and send it to the BTO, with details about when and where you found the bird and, if you can tell, what may have caused its death. They will then send you all the information gathered about the bird when it was originally ringed. Never attempt to remove a ring from the leg of a living bird, as birds' bones are very fragile and can easily be broken.

Photographing birds

Bird photography requires great patience, as well as expensive equipment and considerable technical skill; but, if you can afford it, it is one of the most satisfying activities which an amateur bird-watcher can perform.

The most suitable camera is a single-lens reflex camera, with interchangeable lenses and a through-the-lens metering system. At least one telephoto lens of not less than 200 mm focal length is essential; this will enable you to photograph birds in close-up without alarming them. A tripod and cable release will help to eliminate blurred pictures caused by camera shake.

Remember how easily birds can be disturbed, and never do anything which threatens their welfare. Disturbing birds in the breeding season often causes them to desert their eggs or young, and for certain species the law requires that you have a licence before photographing them at the nest. The Royal Society for the Protection of Birds publishes a booklet, *Wild Birds and the Law,* which lists all the protected species.

Many species of birds are heard more often than they are seen, and in recent years recording bird-song has become an increasingly popular hobby among bird-watchers. As with photography, it is necessary to choose your equipment with great care, and preferably with expert guidance; but even with inexpensive tape-recorders it is possible to achieve many interesting results.

Societies and journals
The best way to make contact with other bird-watchers is to join your local bird-watching society. These societies often organise weekend excursions to nature reserves and sanctuaries, and also have occasional films and lectures presented by experts. These meetings are excellent opportunities to discuss any problems you may have with bird identification or understanding individual bird behaviour, as well as for

gaining advice on the purchase of equipment. The annual bird reports which they publish will give you much useful information about the birds in your own area. Most public libraries can tell you the addresses of local societies, and how to join them.

There are also several national ornithological societies, some of which you may wish to join. The major societies are listed below, together with a selection of their journals.

BRITISH ORNITHOLOGISTS' UNION *c/o The Zoological Society of London, Regent's Park, London NW1 4RY.* One of the world's foremost ornithological societies, chiefly for professional ornithologists, or advanced amateurs. It holds occasional meetings, with lectures or films on any aspect of world ornithology. Publishes *Ibis,* a quarterly journal which contains articles covering a wide range of subjects related to birds.
BRITISH TRUST FOR ORNITHOLOGY *Beech Grove, Station Road, Tring, Hertfordshire.* Similar to the BOU, but deals solely with British birds. Runs the national ringing scheme, the Common Birds Census, and various other educational or research projects. Publishes the journal *Bird Study.*
IRISH WILDBIRD CONSERVANCY *Southview, Church Road, Greystones, Co Wicklow, Ireland.* The Irish equivalent of the BTO.
ROYAL SOCIETY FOR THE PROTECTION OF BIRDS *The Lodge, Sandy, Bedfordshire.* Owns and manages some of the most important nature reserves in Britain. Runs courses for beginners in many parts of the country, and publishes *Birds,* a quarterly magazine dealing with all aspects of bird-watching.

SCOTTISH ORNITHOLOGISTS CLUB *21 Regent Terrace, Edinburgh, Scotland.* Similar aims to the BTO, with particular reference to bird-watching and birdlife in Scotland.
THE WILDFOWL TRUST *Slimbridge, Gloucestershire.* Mainly concerned with the conservation of wildfowl. Manages several important sanctuaries where wild ducks, geese and swans can be observed at close quarters. Publishes *Wildfowl,* an annual report containing articles about wildfowl, and information about the Trust's collection.
ROYAL SOCIETY FOR NATURE CONSERVATION *The Green, Nettleham, Lincoln LN2 2NR.* Parent body of the Nature Conservation Trusts, which manage more than 1,300 reserves, many with facilities for bird-watchers.

The bird-watcher's code
Whatever you choose to do as a bird-watcher – whether you prefer travelling widely to watch birds, or setting up a hide in one place, whether you are photographing, recording or counting birds – there is a code of conduct always to be observed.

Never cause undue disturbance to birds, especially in the breeding season.
Always obtain permission before venturing on to private land.
Keep to paths as far as possible.
Never park so as to block the entrance to a field.
Leave gates as you find them.
Leave no litter.
When you have finished watching a bird, leave quietly in order not to frighten it.

Glossary

A

Accidental Uncommon visitor, arriving only when blown off course or disorientated; same as VAGRANT.

Adult Bird with fully developed final plumage.

Albino Bird with partial or total absence of dark pigment, giving it a white appearance. In a true albino, dark pigment is completely absent from the beak, eyes and legs, as well as from the plumage.

Axillaries Feathers in the axilla, or 'armpit'.

B

Barb Branch of the central shaft of a feather.

Barbule Branch of the BARB of a feather.

Bastard wing Group of feathers at first digit of wing from tip, or 'thumb'.

Blaze Coloured patch at base of bill.

Breeding plumage Plumage developed during the breeding season.

Brood patch Area of featherless, thickened skin on abdomen developed as an aid to incubating eggs.

C

Call Brief sound used for contact within a species, to warn of danger, and so on. Same throughout the year.

Carpal joint Forward-pointing joint of the wing when closed: the 'wrist'.

Cere Fleshy covering at base of bill found in hawks, pigeons and other birds.

Colony Gathering of some species of birds, to breed or roost.

Contour feathers Feathers lying along the body, streamlining it and insulating it against cold.

Coverts Feathers overlying the bases of the tail feathers or major wing feathers; for example tail covert, wing covert, under-wing covert. Also the area of feathers covering a bird's ear (ear covert).

Crepuscular Active only at dusk and dawn.

D

Dialect Local variation in the song of a bird population.

Display Posturing, usually by male bird to attract female during breeding season; also to warn off rival males, and to defend TERRITORY.

Diurnal Active only in daylight hours.

Dorsal Belonging to a bird's back.

Down First feather covering of young birds of some species.

E

Eclipse Post-breeding moult, characteristic of ducks, during which for a short time, males become flightless, lose their bright plumage and come to resemble females.

Egg-tooth Horny protuberance at tip of upper MANDIBLE of a chick, used to crack shell when emerging.

Eruption Mass movement of birds, occurring at irregular intervals.

Escape Species or individual bird escaped or liberated from captivity.

Exotic Term describing a species foreign to an area.

Eye-stripe Distinctively coloured stripe of feathers leading back from or through the eye.

F

Feral Term describing wild bird population that originated in captivity.

First year Period between the time a bird leaves the nest and the following breeding season.

Fore-edge, fore-wing Leading edge of wing.

G

Gape Angle of bill opening.

H

Hawking Capture of flying insects while bird is on the wing.

Hood Area of contrasting plumage covering most of head.

I

Immature Bird in plumage indicating lack of sexual maturity.

Introduced Term describing birds captured in one area and released in another.

Invasion Sudden mass arrival of birds not usually seen in an area.

J

Juvenile Bird in its first covering of true feathers.

L

Lek Place where males of some species, for example black grouse, display communally prior to breeding.

Lore Area between base of upper mandible and eye.

M

Mandible Upper or lower part of bill.

Mantle Back.

Melanistic Term describing a bird with an abnormally large amount of dark pigment in its plumage.

Migrant Species that does not remain on its breeding grounds

throughout the year.
Mob Aggression, usually directed against a predator.
Morph Same as PHASE.
Moustachial stripe Streak of contrasting feathers running back from the base of the bill.

N

Nail Shield or horny plate at tip of upper mandible, found in some geese and ducks.
Nidiculous Term describing young that are hatched helpless and blind, and stay in nest for a considerable time.
Nidifugous Term describing young that are hatched with eyes open, covered with down and able to leave nest almost immediately.
Nocturnal Active only during darkness.

O

Oceanic Another word for PELAGIC.
Orbital ring Fleshy ring around the eye.

P

Partial migrant Species of which some individuals migrate, but others remain on their breeding grounds.
Passage migrant Bird usually breeding and wintering outside an area, but regularly seen on migration.

Pelagic Term describing seabird that seldom or never visits land except in breeding season.
Phase Distinctive variation of plumage within a species.
Preen gland Gland on rump that exudes oil as an aid to preening.
Primary feathers A bird's main flight feathers, attached to 'hand'.

R

Race Term used to describe a subspecies of a bird which inhabits a different region and has slightly different physical characteristics, as for example, plumage pattern.
Raptor Bird of prey, excluding owls.
Resident Bird present throughout year.

S

Scapulars Feathers above the shoulders of a bird.
Secondary feathers Flight feathers attached to 'forearm'.
Sedentary Term describing species that does not migrate or move far from its breeding ground.
Song Language of a bird, intended to identify its TERRITORY to other birds and attract females to intended breeding area.
Speculum Contrasting patch of SECONDARY FEATHERS in wing, usually in ducks.

Spinning Action of some water birds, for example phalaropes, swimming in tight circles to bring food to the surface.
Stoop Term describing dive of a raptor, especially peregrine falcon.
Sub-song Subdued song outside period of full song, or by young males.
Subspecies See RACE.
Superciliary stripe Streak of contrasting feathers above a bird's eye.

T

Tarsus Part of a bird's leg from directly above the toes to the first joint.
Territory Part of a habitat defended by the bird or group of birds occupying it against other birds.

V

Vagrant Uncommon visitor, arriving only when blown off course or disoriented.
Ventral Belonging to a bird's underside or belly.

W

Wattles Fleshy protuberances on head.
Web Flesh between toes of water birds.
Wing-bar Conspicuous stripe across the wing, formed by tips of feathers of contrasting colour.
Wing linings Under-wing COVERTS.
Winter plumage Plumage developed outside breeding season, by male or female bird.
Winter visitor Bird that usually breeds outside the area in which it is seen in winter.

Index

SITES

A
Aberlady Bay 114
Argyll Forest Park 114

B
Bar Mouth 118
Bass Rock 114-115
Blackwater Estuary 107-8
Blakeney 108
Blockhouse Island 117
Bockhill Farm 103
Borrowdale 111
Brecon Beacons 105
Brownsea Island 100-1

C
Caerlaverock 113
Cairngorms 116
Cape Clear Observatory 118
Carneddau 106
Cemlyn 106
Crackington Haven 99-100
Clents Hills 107
Culbin Bar 115-16

D
Derwentwater 111
Dublin Bay 118-19

E
East Head 102
Ennerdale 110-11
Eskdale 109

F
Farne Islands 112

G
Glen Coe 115
Glencoyne 111
Godrevy to Portreath 98-9
Gowbarrow 111
Great Mell Fell 111-12
Green Island 117

H
Hayle Estuary 98

Hentor 100
High Park Estate 108-9
Holnicote Estate 101
Holy Island (Lindisfarne) 112-13

I
Illanmaster 119
Inverpolly 116

L
Lighthouse Island 117
Lindisfarne (Holy Island) 112-13
Little Skellig 118
Lizard Peninsula 98
Lleyn Peninsula 105-6
Long Mynd 107
Longshaw 107
Lord Lonsdale's Commons 110

M
Malham Tarn Estate 109
Marsden Moor 109
Middle Hope 101
Migneint, The 106
Morston 108

N
Newtown Estuary 102
Northey Island 107-8

P
Pagham Harbour 102-3
Pentire Head 99
Port-Eynon 104
Portland Bill 100
Portquin Bay 99
Portreath 98-9
Puffin Island 118

R
Rosemergy Cliffs 98
Rhum, Isle of 115

S
St Abb's Head 113-14

St David's Peninsula 105
Sand Point 101
Sandwich Bay 103
Scafell Group 110
Shell Ness 103-4
Solway Commons 112
Stackpole 104-5
Strangford Lough 117

T
Treavean Cliffs 98
Trowlesworthy Warren 100

W
Wasdale 110
Wexford Slobs 118
Wexford, South 118
Willapark, Tintagel 99
Willings Wall Warren 100
Worm's Head to Port-Eynon 104

BIRDS

B
Bunting, Lapland 95
 Snow 94
buzzard 33

C
capercaillie 41
chough 81
cormorant 20
corncrake 43
crow, carrion 84
curlew 58

D
dipper 85
diver, black-throated 13
 red-throated 12
dotterel 45
dove, stock 77
duck, long-tailed 29
dunlin 54

E
eagle, golden 34
eider 28

F
falcon, peregrine 38
fieldfare 91
flycatcher, pied 87
fulmar 16

G
gannet 19
godwit, bar-tailed 57
goose, barnacle 24
 Brent 23
grebe, black-necked 15
 Slavonian 14
greenshank 55
grouse, black 42
 red 40
guillemot 74
 black 76
gull, black-headed 62

common 64
great black-backed 65
herring 67
lesser black-backed 66

H
harrier, hen 32

J
jackdaw 82

K
kestrel 36
kittiwake 63
knot 50

M
merganser, red-breasted 31
merlin 37

O
osprey 35
ouzel, ring 90
owl, short-eared 78
oystercatcher 44

P
petrel, storm 18
pipit, meadow 79
 rock 80
plover, golden 46
 grey 49
 ringed 47
ptarmigan 39
puffin 75

R
raven 83
razorbill 73
redshank 56
redstart, black 89

S
sanderling 53
sandpiper, common 59

purple 51
scaup 27
scoter, common 30
shag 21
shearwater, Manx 17
shelduck 25
skua, Arctic 60
 great 61
stint, little 52
swan, mute 22

T
tern, Arctic 71
 common 70
 little 72
 roseate 69
 Sandwich 68
tit, crested 92
turnstone 48
twite 93

W
wheatear 88
wigeon 26
wren 86

SEASIDE & MOORLAND BIRDS
is based on the Reader's Digest Field Guide to Birds of Britain to which the
following made major contributions:

CONSULTANTS AND AUTHORS
Dr Philip J.K. Burton, British Museum (Natural History)
Robert Gillmor   Howard Ginn, M.A.
Wildlife Advisory Branch, Nature Conservancy Council
T.W. Parmenter
John Parslow, Director (Conservation), Royal Society for the Protection of Birds
Cyril A. Walker, British Museum (Natural History)
D.I.M. Wallace, B.A.

ARTISTS

Stephen Adams   Hermann Heinzel
Norman Arlott   Mick Loates
Peter Barrett   Sean Milne
Trevor Boyer   Robert Morton
John Busby   D.W. Ovenden
John Francis   Patrick Oxenham
Robert Gillmor   Jim Russell
Tim Hayward   Ken Wood

CARTOGRAPHY
The distribution maps were based on information supplied by John Parslow and
prepared by Clyde Surveys Ltd

Acknowledgements

The editor and publishers would like to thank the following for their invaluable help in compiling information for this book:

Katherine Hearn (Assistant Adviser on Conservation) and Keith Alexander (Surveyor, Biological Survey Team), National Trust.

Graeme Morison of The National Trust for Scotland.

Richard Nairn, Director of the Irish Wild Bird Conservancy.

The British Trust for Ornithology, including many of its local representatives.

Editorial and design
Researched, written and edited by Richard Platt; assistant editor Rosemary Dawe; designed by Arthur Brown; artwork on page 6; map on page 96 by Line and Line.